HIKER'S GUIDE

TO THE HIGH SIERRA

MT. WHITNEY

THIRD EDITION

HIKER'S GUIDE

TO THE HIGH SIERRA

MT. WHITNEY

The Peak and Surrounding Highlands

THIRD EDITION

Thomas Winnett

Drawings by Lucille Winnett

WILDERNESS PRESS
BERKELEY

FIRST EDITION May 1971
SECOND EDITION February 1978
THIRD EDITION July 2001

Cover design by Jaan Hitt
Book design by Archetype
All photos by the author except where otherwise indicated
Front cover photo: *©2001 Thomas Winnett, Harrison Pass*
Back cover photo: *©2001 Thomas Winnett, granite mountains, typical of the High Sierra*
Frontispiece photo: *©2001 Thomas Winnett, Mt. Whitney*

Library of Congress Card Catalog Number 77-77224
International Standard Book Number 0-89997-300-0
Manufactured in the United States

Published by Wilderness Press
1200 5th St.
Berkeley, CA 94710-1306
(800) 443-7227
FAX (510) 558-1696

Write, call, or fax for a free catalog
Check our website for updates and new titles
from Wilderness Press: *www.wildernesspress.com*

Library of Congress Cataloging-in-Publication Data:

Winnett, Thomas.
Mt. Whitney, the peak and surrounding highlands / Thomas Winnett ; drawings by Lucille Winnett.-- 3rd ed.
p. cm. -- (Hiker's guide to the High Sierra)
Rev. ed. of: Mt. Whitney / Wilderness Press. 2nd ed. 1978.
Includes bibliographical references (p.) and index.
ISBN 0-89997-300-0
1. Hiking--California--Whitney, Mount--Guidebooks. 2. Whitney, Mount (Calif.)--Guidebooks. I. Title: Mt. Whitney. II. Title: Mount Whitney, the peak and surrounding highlands. III. Wilderness Press. Mt. Whitney. IV. Title. V. Series.

GV199.42.C22 W458 2001
917.94'86--dc21 2001026327

Wilderness Permit System For the Inyo National Forest

Visit Inyo National Forest on the Web at *www.r5.fs.fed.you/inyo* for the latest INF information. Year-round, you must have a permit to stay overnight in the wilderness. You don't need a permit to dayhike except on the main Mt. Whitney Trail. For trips during the quota period, you can reserve a permit as described below. Outside the quota period and for non-quota trails, you can get a self-issue permit for this area at:

Mt. Whitney Ranger Station (open spring-fall)
(760) 876-6200 / (760) 876-6201 TDD
On U.S. Highway 395 at the south end of Lone Pine

InterAgency Visitor Center — Lone Pine
(open all year)
(760) 876-6222 / (760) 876-6223 TDD
At the intersection of 395 and State Route 136, south of Lone Pine

Trailheads *except* for the Main Mt. Whitney Trail

The quota period is the last Friday in June, through September 15. INF sets aside 60% of the permits for reservations made in advance and 40% for walk-ins.

Permit reservations. Download a permit-reservation application form from the INF website or request one by phone, (760) 873-2400. INF starts accepting applications *with fees* for reserved permits beginning March 1 and up to two days before your date of entry. No fee, no permit. Allow time to receive the reservation letter by mail or ask that it be held for you .

To reserve permits by mail, send the application with fee (below) to:

Inyo National Forest Wilderness Reservation Office
873 N. Main St.
Bishop, CA 93514

To reserve permits by FAX, send the application with fee to (760) 873-2484.

To reserve permits by telephone: INF accepts reservation applications with fees by phone beginning May 1, only from 1–5 p.m. Monday–Friday, at (760) 873-2483.

Fee. $5/person except for any trip that enters the Mt. Whitney Zone (which includes the North Fork of Lone Pine Creek). If your trip enters this zone, then regardless of where it starts on INF, the fee is $15/person. Mailed applications: pay fees by check or money order in U.S. funds, payable to "USDA Forest Service," or pay by Visa or MasterCard. FAX-ed and phoned applications: pay only by Visa or MasterCard.

Permits on demand (walk-ins). On-demand permits are free. For trailheads in this book, you may get a permit beginning at 11 a.m. on the day before your entry date, at the ranger station or visitor center above, if any are left.

Main Mt. Whitney Trail

Dayhikers, including those who hike at night without camping, must have permits to hike beyond the junction with the lateral to Lone Pine Lake. Backpackers must have permits to stay overnight anywhere along the trail. All permits for the Main Mt. Whitney Trail are 100% reservable in advance for both overnight stays and dayhikes. The quota period is May 15–November 1.

Permit reservations. Download the special form and instructions from the INF website or request them from the office in Bishop, (760) 873-2400. Applications are accepted only during February. INF holds a lottery beginning February 15 to determine who gets permits for when. FAX or mail your permit application with fee to the INF Wilderness Reservations Office in Bishop (see above). *Don't apply by phone.* Winners get permit-reservation letters by mail; losers get their applications returned. Expect to hear by April 30.

Fee. $15/person.

Permits on demand (walk-ins). The information is the same as for other trails listed above. Permits are available only if someone cancels a reservation or if there is an unreserved slot on the day you wish to enter—very unlikely.

A permit reservation is not a permit!

To pick up your permit, present your valid permit-reservation letter in person during business hours at the specified ranger station/visitor center. The letter also explains how to make other arrangements.

Owens Valley from Mt. Whitney Trail

Table of Contents

Location of MT. WHITNEY
The Peak and Surrounding Highlands

Introduction

FIRST PUBLISHED IN 1971, the Wilderness Press HIGH SIERRA HIKING GUIDES were the first *complete* guides for hiking and backpacking in the famous California High Sierra. There had long been a great demand for literature about America's favorite wilderness, John Muir's "Range of Light." To meet this demand, we undertook this guide series. Now, 30 years later, Wilderness Press is proud to continue three of our original titles in our renamed HIKER'S GUIDE TO THE HIGH SIERRA series. These classics are *the* source for information on many of California's favorite high country destinations in the Yosemite, Tuolumne Meadows, and Mt. Whitney areas.

In this book, we have included a new geologic section by Jeffrey Schaffer, revised chapters on flora and on fauna (thanks to the United States Department of Forestry), as well as trail updates, made possible in part because of the contributions of readers over the years. If you spot any errors or out-of-date information, please contact us by email: *mail@wildernesspress.com.*

The purpose of each book in the series is threefold: first, to provide a reliable basis for planning a trip; second, to serve as a field guide while you are on the trail; and third, to stimulate you to further field investigation and background reading. In each guide, there are a minimum of 100 described miles of trails, and the descriptions are supplemented with an area location map, trail profiles and other logistical and background information. As with all Wilderness Press titles, books in the HIKER'S GUIDE TO THE HIGH SIERRA series are based on first-hand observation and experience. There is absolutely no substitute for walking the trails, so the authors have walked all the trails, in some cases many times over.

Maps

Each guide originally covered one 15-minute U.S.G.S. topographic quadrangle, an area about 13 miles east-west by 17 miles north-south. The U.S.G.S. no longer produces the 15-minute maps and has replaced them with 7.5-minutes maps available through local outdoor and sports retailers, or map sellers, such as The Map Center in Berkeley, California (510) 841-6277, as well as through the U.S.G.S. itself.

Four 7.5′ U.S.G.S. topographic maps cover the Mt. Whitney region, replacing the old 15′ topo. Imagine a rectangle divided into quarters. The Mt. Brewer 7.5′ topo map covers the northwest quarter; the Mt. Williamson 7.5′ topo map covers the northeast quarter; the Mt. Kaweah 7.5′ topo map covers the southwest quarter and the Mt. Whitney 7.5′ topo map covers the southeast quarter. The map located to the east of the Mt. Whitney 7.5′ topo map is Mt. Langley. It is outside of the area covered by the Mt. Whitney 15′ topo map but has the trailhead on it.

Map information is available from:

The Map Center
2440 Bancroft Way
Berkeley, CA 94704
(510) 841-6277 (phone)
(510) 841-0858 (fax)
email: *themapcenter@aol.com*

The Country

MOST PEOPLE WHO COME to the Mt. Whitney area in the southern Sierra Nevada mountain range do so in order to climb Mt. Whitney. In coming only for this purpose, they miss out on some of the finest mountain experiences to be had anywhere in the world. This region contains the highest, wildest parts of the entire High Sierra. Only one road is shown anywhere on the map, and it barely pierces the northeast boundary. A gigantic horseshoe of 13,000′ and 14,000′ peaks protects the heart of this area from the incursions of casual campers and day-walkers.

Inside the horseshoe is the high plateau where the Kern River has its sources. Like an equine foot, this horseshoe is cleft down its center by the great trench of the Kern River, as deep as Yosemite Valley, not much wider, and very much longer. The erosive power of water and ice found a receptive channel here along a great, straight-line earthquake fault in the earth's crust. The Kern River, unlike all other Sierra Nevada rivers, which flow *west* down the slope from the crest, flows south for over 70 miles before finally finding a way over to the San Joaquin Valley, where its waters are diverted into irrigation ditches.

On the east side of the horseshoe is the climax of the Sierra crest, with four 14,000′ peaks, from Mt. Tyndall on the north to Mt. Muir on the south. The top of the horseshoe is the Kings-Kern divide, notched by Forester Pass, the last and highest pass along the John Muir Trail for those walking south. The western arm of the horseshoe, culminating in 13,802′ Mt. Kaweah, seals off this Shangri-La basin from the lower, gentler western Sierra slopes.

Only five maintained trails give access to this wilderness, and of these only three cross the great horseshoe anywhere around its arc. But the lover of high country does not lobby for more trail-building, and often prefers to enter the upper Kern Basin via some favorite cross-country route hidden among the granite pinnacles and talus slopes. Lovers of high country rate the Mt. Whitney area "tops" and, if you can ignore the claims of that distant state acquired from the Russians, it is indeed the top of the United States.

Mt. Whitney over a church, Lone Pine

The History

THE YEAR WAS 1864, the place was the uncharted Sierra wilderness.

> To the south, more than eight miles away, a wall of peaks stood across the gulf, dividing the Kings, which flowed north at your feet, from the Kern River, that flowed down the trough in the opposite direction.
>
> I did not wonder that Brewer and Hoffman pronounced our undertaking impossible; but when I looked at Cotter there was such complete bravery in his eye that I asked him if he was ready to start. His old answer, "Why not?" left the initiative with me; so I told Professor Brewer that we would bid him good bye. Our friends helped us on with our packs in silence, and as we shook hands there was not a dry eye in the party. Before he let go of my hand, Professor Brewer asked me for my plan, and I had to own that I had but one, which was to reach the highest peak in the range.

The writer was Clarence King, the peak was Mt. Whitney, and King did reach the top, but only nine years later, after he had climbed two peaks, each of which he thought to be the highest until after he had climbed it.

Clarence King was a member of the California State Geological Survey, an intrepid mountaineer, and a writer of hair-raising prose. The survey, created by the State Legislature in 1860, was under the direction of Josiah D. Whitney. A field trip to the uncharted southern Sierra in 1864 was under the leadership of William Brewer; Charles Hoffman was the cartographer, King and James Gardiner were assistant geologists, and Dick Cotter was their packer.

King and Cotter entered the Mt. Whitney quadrangle (as described on the original U.S.G.S. 15′ topo) on the northwest, at the saddle south of Mt. Brewer, and thus began the region's first recorded exploration. They crossed the mighty Kings-Kern Divide, risking their lives in the doing, somewhere in the headwaters of East Creek. No one knows exactly where, but an educated guess is the saddle immediately east of Thunder Mountain.

Once over this divide, they set out for Mt. Tyndall, named by King when he arrived at its summit. But then he saw there were two peaks higher than this one. They were, of course, Mt. Williamson and Mt. Whitney. Of the latter, King said, "That which looked highest of all was a cleanly cut helmet of granite, lying about six miles south. Mount Whitney, as we afterwards called it in honor of our chief, is probably the highest land within the United States. The summit looks glorious, but inaccessible."

Since their provisions and Cotter's shoes were both about gone, they returned to Brewer's camp in the Roaring River watershed. King, however, was obsessed with climbing Whitney. A few days later, he set off from Visalia and crossed the range to a point south of Whitney and east of the main crest. After several days of exploration in unmapped, unknown, extremely rugged country, King got to within three or four hundred feet of the summit before being defeated. Again he called the summit "inaccessible."

The work of the Survey kept King away from the Whitney area for the next few years, but in June 1871 he was himself in charge of a geological survey. While returning to his party in Wyoming from San Francisco, he detoured south to Lone Pine for another chance at the unclimbed giant. And, via a new route, he gained the summit. At last he had his first ascent, and the accolades it brought him.

Two years later a scientist by the name of W.A. Goodyear proved simply and conclusively that King had been, not on Whitney, but on a peak about 6 miles south — now called Mt. Langley. The real Whitney, which King had seen from Tyndall, remained unclimbed. King, getting the news in the East, immediately set out for California. This time he did indeed reach the summit of the real Mt. Whitney. But as he discovered in records he found on top, he was not the first.

A mere 13 days after Goodyear had made his statement, on August 18, 1873, three fishermen had climbed Whitney, from their base camp at Soda Springs on the Kern River. Little publicized since, they were John Lucas,

Charles Begole, and Albert Johnson. Late in August a second party surmounted the highest peak, and in early September a third. King came on September 19.

Just a month later came a man now more familiar than King or any other Sierra explorer: John Muir. As usual, he went alone, finding a route up a couloir on the northeast side.

By 1881, the summit was being used for scientific observations, but staying all night on the summit even in August was too arduous, and the party's leader said a permanent shelter would have to be constructed. A stock trail was needed, too, which the citizens of Lone Pine completed in 1904. The stone structure that stands on Whitney today was built in 1909, and scientists made expeditions to the summit in 1909, 1910, and 1913. Since then, other high places, such as Pikes Peak, have been made more easily accessible, and scientists on Whitney these days are there for nonprofessional reasons — although they are not above sleeping in the shelter if they choose to spend the night on top.

Of course, Mt. Whitney peak is no longer the highest in the U.S. — McKinley is. And the often-read statement that it is now second highest is wrong by 14 peaks; there are 15 higher in Alaska.

The west "half" of the zero-dimensional pinpoint that theoretically marks the summit of Mt. Whitney is in Sequoia National Park, and has been since 1926. The park was created in the same year as Yosemite, 1890, but it was much smaller until Congress in 1926 added the part that is in the Kern River watershed.

Exploration of the rest of the Mt. Whitney area languished from the time Brewer's party left until roughly the 1890s, when early Sierra Club people, having worked their way, summer by summer, south from Yosemite reached the Kings-Kern Divide. Bolton Coit Brown, a Professor of Drawing at Stanford, scrambled over the peaks and ridges here, sketching and mapping what he saw. For years, his sketches were the only useful maps of some of the area. With his wife Lucy he went over the pass which bears her name, and she seems to have gone just about everywhere he did. On their third summer-long trip, they brought their two-year-old daughter on a mule.

In 1908 Joseph N. LeConte and two companions took pack animals from Tuolumne Meadows to the South Fork of the Kings River via a route that the present John Muir Trail more or less follows. This super-trail was completed in 1938 with the building of the Mather Pass segment, but by 1932, with the opening of Forester Pass, there was a continuous, maintained route from Yosemite Valley to Mt. Whitney.

The future of the Mt. Whitney area is conjectural. Most of it is so remote that overuse would seem to be far in the future. But backpacking in the Sierra in recent years has grown at a great rate, and some kind of control has become necessary. One obvious way to preserve the wilderness is to limit access, using required permits as the device. Permits have become a reality. Another kind of control would involve building facilities such as rest rooms and restaurants. The Forest Service might even seek to remove the Mt. Whitney trail from its present wilderness status, in order to permit some construction.

There is always some question whether it is possible by definition to "manage a wilderness." Better alternatives must exist, and it behooves dedicated backpackers to think through them, and propose their best ideas to all who will listen.

Mountain Chickadee

The Geology

WHEN YOU APPROACH the Mt. Whitney area via Highway 395 through the Owens Valley, you are astounded and awestruck by the sheer, towering, grand eastern scarp of the Sierra. How could such a fabulous scarp have been created?

A long-ignored part of the answer lies beneath the highway. The valley's sediments are thousands of feet thick, locally as much as 7000′, putting the top of the valley's buried bedrock as much as 3000′ below sea level. It got there through thousands of feet of down faulting, this mostly occurring, along with volcanism, in the last 3–4 million years. But that's only part of the answer. Obviously, the Sierra rose, but when? Until the 1990s, virtually everyone agreed that it rose in the Nevadan orogeny, a mountain-building period centered around 160 million years ago, and that a long period of erosion then ensued, followed by another round of mountain building over the last 1-20+ million years (estimates vary).

The new millennium interpretation is quite different. There were two early periods where marine sediments and/or underlying continental crust were compressed and highlands developed; these periods centered around 350–365 and 240–250 million years ago. The latest mountain-building period, formerly called the Nevadan orogeny, was most intense about 152–163 million years ago, but it existed for considerably longer, starting about 180 million years ago, if not earlier, and lasting until 140 million years ago, if not much later.

During each mountain-building period, previous sedimentary and volcanic rocks were changed, respectively, into metasedimentary and metavolcanic rocks in response to intense pressure, great heat, and circulating corrosive fluids. In the Mt. Whitney area, the only remaining metamorphic rocks occur in two linear vestiges, both originally volcanic, but now phyllite and schist. One remnant is in the trail-less southwest part from Lake 10875

Naked granite peaks of the southern Sierra

southeast along the lower northeast slopes of Red Spur to the brink of Kern Canyon. The other extends discontinuously southward through the northeast. No trail crosses it, but the observant hiker may see small vestiges on slopes south and west above Mahogany Flat, along the Shepherd Pass Trail.

The metamorphic rocks make up only 2% of the region's bedrock; granitic rocks make up the rest. Granitic rocks are igneous *intrusive* rocks, ones that solidified within Earth's crust. These originated from partial melting of a descending plate at depths of 60+ miles. The melt, or *magma*, rose and mostly solidified a few or more miles beneath Earth's surface to form bodies of granitic rock, called *plutons*. Some of the melt reached the surface, typically along faults, to erupt and create volcanic, or igneous *extrusive*, rocks. Almost all our area's granitic rocks formed between about 80–120 million years ago, and the bulk of them between 80–85 million years ago, during the late Cretaceous heyday of the dinosaurs, when tyrannosaurids terrorized the continents. What the dinosaurs would have seen was a volcanic range, similar to the modern Andes, having a tropical climate but snow-capped peaks up to 20,000+′. The Owens Valley may have resembled the Andes' Altiplano and could have been 10,000–15,000′ high, and the White Mountains mirrored the Sierra in height and composition.

The entire landscape began to fall apart, literally, about 80 million years ago. Beneath Earth's brittle, *upper* continental crust is a ductile, *lower* continental crust. Ductile materials can slowly flow, and when a mountain range reaches Andean heights, the lower crust begins to flow laterally, undermining the range. The upper continental crust, being brittle, cannot flow, and so it is torn apart along its base. This subhorizontal rift plane is called a detachment (fault), and the upper crust of the early range was transported away, being eroded in a process that may have taken a few million years.

With the upper few miles of the early range removed, including almost all of the metamorphic rocks, the lower crust rose upward to about its present heights, exposing the formerly buried plutons. Today's broad summits, such as Mt. Whitney and Diamond Mesa, haven't changed much in the last 80 million years, being lowered through weathering and erosion by only a few hundred feet, if that. Not so for the remaining lands. Over tens of millions of years the modern drainage patterns formed, including impressively deep, arrow-straight Kern Canyon, which originated along a fault that developed as the dinos were going extinct about 65 million years ago.

By 2½ million years ago, when serious glaciation first developed in the Sierra, the range had taken on a modern look. You won't see any evidence for this in the Mt. Whitney area; most lies north of Yosemite. However, if you were to explore the lands around Kern Peak to the south, you'd see remnants of cinder cones and basalt (lava) flows, the oldest cone being Little Whitney Cone. At about ¾ million years old, parts of the cone and its flow still existed, despite being repeatedly glaciated. At best the granitic flats and gentle slopes have lost a foot or so since this volcano erupted.

Within the Mt. Whitney quadrangle, virtually all of the landscape has been glaciated, except for the high peaks and ridges and the lower lands in the northeast corner. Glaciers have performed two significant feats. First, they quarried the fractured bedrock to create bedrock basins, which then filled to become lakes some 13,000+ years ago, when the last of the major glaciers retreated into oblivion. Were it not for these lakes, perhaps only serious mountaineers would visit this area.

Second, glaciers transported tremendous amounts of rockfall, which is derived in part through freeze and thaw of jointed rock, but mostly through earthquakes, such as the 1872 Owens Valley earthquake, centered around Lone Pine, in which the valley sank a few feet. As you ascend the Sierra's east slopes, you will see accumulations of rockfall — *talus* — waiting to be transported in the next round of glaciation. As rocks fall from steep slopes, canyons widen, giving them the broad floors typically ascribed to glacial erosion, which is minimal. At heads of canyons, widening through rockfall is especially prominent, creating amphitheater-like bowls called *cirques.* Two cirques backwasting on opposite sides of a divide eventually transform it into a knifelike ridge called an *arête*; three or more create a spiry peak called a *horn.*

A final round of glaciation, the Little Ice Age, began around 1400 AD, but perhaps due to the Industrial Revolution and the greenhouse gases it produced, this minor glaciation then waned after the mid-1800s. As we continue to warm the atmosphere with these gases, snowfall will diminish, and native plants and animals will be stressed by a rapidly changing climate. In particular, the alpine plant community, the subject of "The Flora" chapter, will diminish as foxtail and whitebark pines encroach ever higher into their realm.

Let you, while waiting for new
monuments, preserve the
old monuments . . .

—Victor Hugo

The Fauna

THIS GUIDE WILL ACQUAINT YOU with some of the animals you may meet in the neighborhood of Mt. Whitney, but is by no means comprehensive.

The remote country of Mt. Whitney is one of the last places in the world where one might still see a **wolverine**. Endangered by the encroachment of humans and loss of habitat, the species has nonetheless persisted in proportion to their endurance, tenacity and ferocity: indeed, wolverines might once have inherited the earth. Bears and mountain lions, even when in pairs, have been seen to back away from their meal and yield possession of it to an approaching wolverine. Yet, this animal is no longer than a poodle, and not so tall. A large one weighs but 30 pounds. Zoologists can't completely explain their power. Short bones, thick muscles, and a stocky build probably have something to do with their strength. Some have mentioned thyroid glands or adrenaline secretion, but very tentatively. Perhaps it will remain unexplained, except in the heart of the wolverine.

A member of the weasel family, the wolverine has evolved into a chunky, powerful animal capable of traveling long and far through deep snow. It can live in such a

Wolverine

harsh environment that it has almost no competitors, the climate itself being the chief enemy. When the snow lies deep, and the small rodents are hibernating under it, the wolverine must range far and wide to get enough food to survive, and he must eat anything, dead or alive, that he can find. He must also be able to go for long periods without eating, and so has developed such an ability to gorge himself that some people call him the "glutton."

If you should be so lucky as to see a wolverine, you would probably not mistake him for anything else, except possibly a young bear. However, his legs are shorter than a bear's, and the tail is large and bushy. Mostly brownish black, he has two big brownish-gray stripes extending from the shoulders to the base of the tail, and a gray bar across the forehead. More likely — but not commonly — you might see the wolverine's tracks. They may look like the tracks of a coyote or a mountain lion if the fifth toe on the forefoot hasn't made a clear impression.

A mammal you are much more likely to see or hear, due to their bleating squeak, is the **pika**, also known as a **cony**. Having the head of a rat, the body and fur of a rabbit, and no visible tail, the pika presents a curious appearance. You find it at elevations of 8000–12,000′, living in colonies. One colony was observed living in a rock slide covering more than an acre of ground, a conglomerated mass many feet deep, with blocks of rock ranging from a few inches to many feet in diameter, though providing ample shelter with many crevices as runways. Among the cracks of this slide pikas have built their homes, and they forage for herbs and grasses growing around nearby lakes. The lower part of the slide extends well out into the lake, so the animals can obtain drink during the winter without exposing themselves on top of the snow to bad weather or predators.

Pikas are of social and affectionate disposition, and notwithstanding their wild, free life on the edge of treeline in the solitudes of the High Sierra, they seem to be holding their own and increasing in number. Their haymaking season is between August 20 and September 15, varying somewhat with altitude and the ripening condition of the grasses. Practically all members of the colony take part in the harvest. The one object is to store sufficient hay to last over the winter. This is no small task, as the winters often last eight months, and snow is 10–30′ deep over all vegetation. The pikas with their strong incisor teeth cut off the grass close to the roots and then place it carefully in small bunches for drying. Then they take the sheaves of hay, throw them over their shoulders, and drag them to the "haybarns" under the rocks. With their snouts and front feet, the little animals force the sheaves of cured grass back into crevices. From the appearance of the hayfield after the harvest season, some people believe that the animals shear off more grass than they want, but the remains are usually hay that has been damaged in the curing process by mountain storms.

The pika is quite agile, and can run like a rat and jump like a rabbit. In bounding from rock to rock when closely pursued, they can spring several feet, though only 7″ long. They hate to get into deep water, but can swim fast for up to 60′ in an emergency. They are home-loving with little migratory impulse other than to search for fresh pasture when unfavorable forage conditions arise or find a new home when forced abroad by congested living conditions. Their worst enemies are the weasel and some hawks.

Once you see these animals you'll have a desire for more acquaintance, for the little cliff-dwellers are curious and interesting from many points of view. Their industry excels that of most animals; they are home-loving, always living in family groups; the sexes are almost alike in size and color; they do not hibernate. Pikas have been able to survive in habitats that are too challenging for many other species of animal.

The **long-tailed weasel** in its white winter coat is sometimes called ermine, but "ermine" is also the name of the **short-tailed weasel**, or **least weasel**, the smallest carnivore in the Sierra. The ermine is a little animal not much bigger than a big mouse, drab-brown upper body, black-tipped tail, and white under-parts and feet. It is about 9″ long overall, of which about 2″ is tail. Like the long-tailed weasel, the short-tailed weasel also turns white in winter. It makes its den in a tiny burrow under a rock or tree and inhabits the Sierra above 6000′ up to treeline. Like so many other mammals, the weasel is rarely seen.

It is difficult to imagine the capacity for predation shown by this animal; its marked intelligence crowns the diminutive weasel as the king of all rodent-killers in the Sierra. One female with six young was observed for 27 days, during which she killed 78 mice, 27 gophers, 2 moles, 34 chipmunks, 3 wood rats and 4 ground squirrels.

The **bighorn sheep**, once widespread in the Sierra, is now found mainly in four rather small areas near the crest in the southern High Sierra. One of these is around Mt. Williamson; the sheep living there are called the Mt. Williamson herd.

Bighorn Sheep

In 1966 the California bighorn sheep *(Ovis canadensis)* was classified as a rare animal within the continental United States. The classification was based largely on a zoologist's 1948–49 studies of the animals in which he found about 390 sheep in five herds in the Sierra. In the late 1960s the Forest Service conducted extensive field surveys on the sheep ranges to determine what changes had occurred since earlier studies. It found that the number of bighorn sheep had declined steadily — although the Mt. Williamson herd had remained fairly static. More recently the herd dwindled greatly. The Forest Service said the factors limiting the size of bighorn herds were forage competition on the winter range with deer and tule elk, and particularly the great increase in human use on the bighorn ranges.

In 1971 the Forest Service created a California bighorn sheep zoological area of two separate pieces: a total of 40,400 acres on the east slopes of Mt. Williamson and of Mt. Baxter (the home of the Mt. Baxter herd). To give top priority to protecting the bighorn sheep, the Forest Service has not built new trails in the area and has maintained existing trails only minimally. In some parts of the area, human travel is restricted and overnight camping is prohibited. The area has been withdrawn from mineral entry, and other regulations have been imposed to help protect these last refuges of these marvelous rare animals. The backpacker can do his bit for *Ovis canadensis* by learning observing the regulations. Inyo National Forest officials can inform you about them.

In January 2000, the U.S. Fish and Wildlife Service listed the Sierra Nevada bighorn sheep as an "endangered species." The population has declined by approximately 90 percent over the last century. Area closures for dogs and domestic goats have been developed to protect habitat and prevent the spread of disease from domestic animals. If you have a wilderness permit reservation for an affected trail, and hope to bring your dog, please contact the ranger station closest to your entry or exit trail to determine if your path is within a closed area.

On the trail to Milestone Bowl

The Flora

YOU WILL PASS THROUGH a number of plant communities as you climb into this region. From Owens Valley, you drive past **sagebrush**, then begin your hike among **pinyon pines** and **mountain mahogany**. Higher up come **Jeffrey pine**, then **western white pine** and **red fir** (the fir being the commonest species if you are ascending north through Kern Canyon).

In the subalpine realm, you encounter **lodgepole pine**, which are common, as well as **limber** and **foxtail pine**, which are not. Limber pine is never common; it prefers high and dry slopes so it thrives in the Sierra's rainshadow. On the other hand, this area is foxtail-pine central; most of the Sierra's foxtails grow here. Although scattered groves of foxtail-pine can also be found in the Klamath Mountains, the majority of the world's specimens grow in the Mt. Whitney quadrangle. Foxtail pines compete with **whitebark pines** for the highest elevations; the treeline is situated roughly at 11–12,000′ elevation. Above that is the realm of the alpine flora. Since this area contains the highest alpine lands of the entire Sierra, it is a fantastic place to see alpine wildflowers. Some favorites include:

Polemonium, or **sky pilot** *(Polemonium eximium)*. One has to climb very high to find this beautiful plant, for it grows far above treeline, and seldom below 11,500′, on the high peaks of the Sierra Nevada crest from Tuolumne County to Tulare and Inyo counties.

Intoxicating perfume permeates the thin air where sky pilot grows upright and tall despite the extreme physical conditions it must live under. Its loosely clustered multiple flowers, source of the perfume, are a luminous blue. The plant is justly famous among Sierra Club members as a symbol of mountaineering achievement, and tradition once decreed that one very tiny sprig of this lovely plant might be picked and worn in the hatband of the mountaineer who had climbed a peak of 13,000′ or higher.

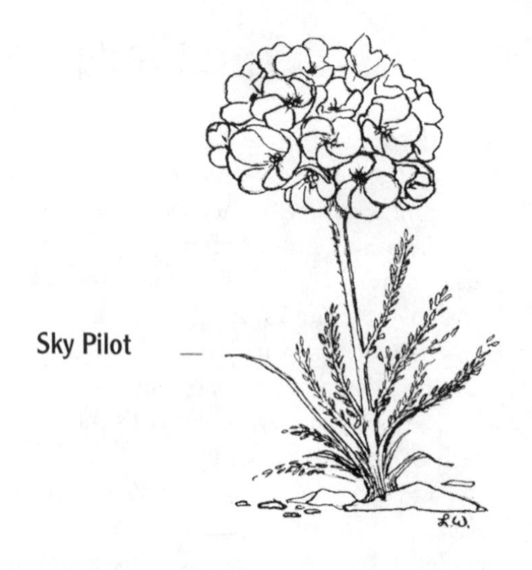

Sky Pilot

Alpine gold, or **alpine sunflower** *(Hulsea algida)*. Alpine gold, along with sky pilot, grows tall and straight on the summits of the Sierra's highest peaks, where other plants lie prostrate and clinging to the scant shelter of the exposed rocky substratum. What a pair! Sky pilot and alpine gold! The gloriously golden color of Hulsea's huge sunflower heads contrasts vividly with the intense blue of sky pilot's flowers. Nature, however, has distributed both of these magnificent plants sparingly. They occur on

Alpine Gold

almost every high peak, yet the individual plants are scattered and often quite distant from one another. Hulsea, unlike sky pilot, ranges far beyond the Sierra into other western alpine areas, but its charm for the Sierra mountaineer is, nonetheless, second only to sky pilot's.

Alpine phlox (*Phlox condensata, P. dispersa,* and *P. pulvinata*). Three alpine species of varying distributions occur above treeline. In this area, the most restricted is the matted *Phlox dispersa*, or High Sierra phlox, which has long rhizomes (horizonatal, buried stems) that give rise to dense tufts of leaves. *Phlox pulvinata*, or carpet phlox, also occurs in highlands east to the Rocky Mountains, and it likewise is matted, but has short rhizomes, and so has closer spaced tufts. Finally, there's *Phlox condensata*, or cushion phlox, which occurs in much of the Sierra's alpine lands. The cushion phlox in particular is a good example of what German botanists call "polster" (cushion) plants. Quite unrelated kinds of arctic and alpine plants living under the severe conditions of high latitude or high altitude frequently have this same type of growth. The heavy, woody roots of polster plants, including those of alpine phloxes, may grow to an amazing length and size, anchoring the plant against the violent winds, and extending deep and wide to gather the scant moisture so vital for combating the desiccating influences of the dry air and low temperatures. These roots also furnish storage

Alpine Phlox

space for reserve food to tide the plant over the long winter season of dormancy. Yet all that appears above ground may be a small, dense mat of leaves and stems pressed together very tightly into a ball or cushion, perhaps only one or two inches high.

No icy gale can tear so much as a leaf from a well-armored polster plant, nor penetrate that armor and still have any strength left. In a relenting mood, however, nature frequently supplies such a sternly frocked plant with a myriad of beautiful blossoms during its brief flowering season. This is what happens to your alpine phloxes. The plant may be quite literally covered with small, exquisite, white or pale lavender flowers, and not a harsh leaf or stem be seen beneath this delicate and wonderfully fragrant mound.

The Climate

WEATHER IS AS IMPORTANT to a backpacker as cards are to a gambler. And in fact it is something of a gamble whether one's trip will be sunny and clear, or wet and cold. Fortunately, in the Mt. Whitney area, the odds are very much in one's favor.

The Sierra Nevada has indisputably the finest climate of any mountain range in America. Only 3% of the year's precipitation falls during the summer. As for warmth, the average daily maximum at 10,000′ in summertime is only about 60° — but no one experiencing the delicious warmth of the direct sunlight in the high country believes that, unless he consults a thermometer. At night in the summer, the temperature usually drops to 40° or less, and freezes are not uncommon but the dryness of the air (augmented by a good sleeping bag) minimizes the feeling of cold. Many High Sierra veterans, in fact, prefer a little frost to wake up to; lying in the sack watching the bright early sun play on a whitened granite slope or meadow is an ineffable experience.

When a thunderstorm does come to Mt. Whitney, the lightning which generally precedes and follows the storm is a danger to be reckoned with. The best rule of thumb in such situations is to avoid being conspicuous and avoid being near conspicuous landmarks. A dense grove of uniformly sized trees is a good place. The most dangerous places are on ridges, under lone trees, and on or beside open expanses of water. Climbers working on exposed surfaces should keep a particularly wary eye on the weather.

But to precede the traveler's visit to Mt. Whitney with dire warnings and a list of do's and don't's is to destroy that prized and terribly fragile element of the wilderness experience called *discovery.* You go to wilderness to discover what is there to be seen and felt; you abandon your defenses against the machines that you left back in Gross

Domestic Productland, and listen to the silence. In a few days, you get an inkling of what things matter.

Great Western Divide from Bighorn Plateau

Survival is not enough. Seeing the Milky Way, experiencing the fragrance of spring, and observing other forms of life continue to play an immense role in the development of humanness.

— Rene Dubos

The Trails

THE MOST USED TRAILS in this area lead to the top of Mt. Whitney — the John Muir Trail coming from the north, and the Mt. Whitney Trail coming from the east. The two are superimposed for their last two miles. Although no figures are available, approximately 90% of the walking mileage in this area can be logged on these two trails. The High Sierra Trail and the East Creek Trail probably account for more than half of the remaining 10%.

While one cannot deny the appeal and the excitement of these trails, one may want to seek a quieter, less traveled piece of country. For this, Mt. Whitney is extremely well suited. Above treeline, you can see for miles, so routes can be especially easy. Furthermore, there are fairly large areas of high plateau, where grades are easy. It is possible to spend a month in the high country, every night at a different campsite if you choose, with little likelihood of seeing anyone else except perhaps from a distance. The authors once spent a week just a mile across gentle slopes from the Muir Trail and saw no one.

Since much of the fun of going cross-country comes from finding your way, the cross-country routes in the descriptions that follow are pointed out only in very general terms. If you have had sufficient experience, you will, with the aid of the topographic maps and some advance planning, get where you want to go. A word of caution is in order here: beginners must err on the conservative side while they get the feel of going cross-country and camping off-trail, and they certainly should not do it alone.

The route descriptions that follow often mention "ducks" and "cairns." A duck is one or several small rocks placed upon a larger rock in such a way that the placement is obviously not natural. A cairn is a number of small rocks made into a pile.

Wood fires are prohibited above 10,000′ in Kings Canyon National Park and above 11,200′ in Sequoia National Park.

THE TRAILHEADS

Symmes Creek Roadend. (Access to Shepherd Pass and Junction Pass.) Go 4.5 miles west from Independence on the Onion Valley Road; turn left at Foothill Road, and go 1.3 miles to a fork. Take the right-hand fork and go past an old corral on the left; immediately cross Symmes Creek. In ½ mile take the right fork, and take the right fork again at the next two forks. Go ½ mile to the trailhead near Symmes Creek. Some of these forks may have small signs.

Whitney Portal. (Access to Mt. Whitney and the John Muir Trail.) At the end of a 13-mile paved road that goes west from Lone Pine.

Cedar Grove. (Access to Bubbs Creek Trail and thence to Trail #5.) Road's end of State 180, through Kings Canyon National Park, 85 miles east of Fresno.

Tom Winnett standing on John Muir Trail at Forester Pass

Trail Descriptions

TRAIL #1
John Muir Trail (31.8 miles)

This long traverse of the Mt. Whitney 15 minute quadrangle is the climax of the John Muir Trail, terminating at the highest point in the "lower 48" states. You begin the trail description at Vidette Meadow on Bubbs Creek, to the north. From Vidette Meadow the trail makes an initial steep ascent and then resolves into a steady climb along the east bank of the creek, through a moderate forest cover of lodgepole pine and occasional foxtail pine. Several campsites line Bubbs Creek, and some around 10,000′ offer fine campsite views of University Peak to the east, Center Peak to the southeast, and East Vidette to the west.

From those campsites, the trail continues up the east side of dashing Bubbs Creek, passing more campsites bunched around small side streams and then reaching the Center Basin/Junction Pass Trail. Just beyond, the Center Basin outlet stream is a formidable ford in early season. Your route then ascends somewhat steeply over nearly barren granite west of towering Center Peak. This climb takes the panting hiker above treeline as it winds back and forth over the runoff stream that drains Lake 12248. Over your shoulder, the peaks of the Sierra crest march away on the northern horizon.

After fording just below Lake 12248, the trail doubles back north on the barren canyon wall and then turns south and soon switchbacks steeply up to a narrow notch in the Kings-Kern Divide called Forester Pass (13,120′), the highest pass on the Muir Trail. Views from this windy notch are extraordinary. The entire Palisade Crest is in view to the northwest. To the north and east are Mt. Pinchot, University Peak, Mt. Bradley, and Mt. Keith. In the south (reading clockwise) are Mt. Guyot, Mt. Kaweah and

Mt. Guyot from Bighorn Plateau

the Kaweah Peaks Ridge, the Red Spur, Kern Point, Black Kaweah, and Red Kaweah.

Leaving this windy notch behind, the trail descends steeply by numerous switchbacks, some of which are mere shelves carved into the steep face of Junction Peak's west shoulder. A few hardy flowers called polemonium and alpine gold share the high slope with scurrying pikas, also known as "conies," (for descriptions see "Flora" and "Fauna" sections in the front of this book). The traveler who looks up is sometimes treated to the sight of a golden eagle soaring high above the granite peaks.

After the trail becomes less steep, your rocky route winds among a number of unnamed, rockbound lakes at the headwaters of Tyndall Creek. Some of these lakes may still be frozen in August. To the east the unusual formation called Diamond Mesa appears as a sheer-walled, flat-topped ridge protruding from the jumbled heights of

Junction Peak. Even here, the barren rock is relieved by occasional flowers of yellow ivesia, red mountain heather, and lavender pussypaws, and marmots hop to their dens as you approach.

Near treeline, your route passes a trail that soon splits, the two branches leading to Lake South America and to Milestone Creek. A short descent brings you to a series of heavily used campsites strung out along Tyndall Creek.

Then you ford the creek (difficult in early season) and soon pass a junction with a trail leading down the valley of Tyndall Creek to the Kern River. In a few more steps, you reach a junction with the Shepherd Pass Trail. Beyond this second junction, your route ascends moderately on a rocky slope under a broken forest cover of lodgepole pines. At Tyndall Frog Ponds, northeast of Tawny Point, there are good campsites and great views, and unfreezing swimming.

As you pass through the immense talus slope of Tawny Point, the tree cover changes to foxtail pine, a fascinating species found mainly in the high southern Sierra near treeline. From here, a gentle, sandy ascent leads to a barely perceptible summit on Bighorn Plateau. About ½ mile

Unnamed lake near Tawny Point

before the summit, you can look south along the crest of the Tyndall Creek glacier's lateral moraine. (The moraine even shows up on the topo map, as a compressed **Z**-curve on the 11,200′ contour line.) The view from the trail approaching Bighorn Plateau is one of the finest along the entire Muir Trail, and photographers may want to snap a series of frames that scan the horizon from Mt. Kaweah to Junction Peak, later to assemble them into a 180° panorama. The unnamed lake on the summit of the plateau, lying west of the trail across a grassy field, is itself quite photogenic in the morning hours. From the summit the hiker southbound on the Muir Trail has a first view of the terminus of this famous trail — Mt. Whitney.

From this plateau the sandy trail descends via several steps to the glacial moraine that covers the valley of Wright Creek. In the meadow you overlook, a trail of use can be found which goes up the watershed to a dozen high, wild lakes. The highest lake is especially recommended for both fishing and beauty. It is a classic cirque lake, close under 14,000′ Mt. Tyndall. However, there is no wood. Fair campsites may be found about 1½ miles downstream from the highest lake in a grove of foxtail pines. When you walk back down this valley, you are tracing the route Clarence King took on his descent from Mt. Tyndall.

Another cross-country route also starts here — the shortcut to the Wallace Creek Trail. The route turns east from the Muir Trail at the west moraine in Wright Creek valley, crosses a little meadow, goes through a saddle in a moraine on the east side of the valley, and then heads toward the cascades of Wallace Creek, visible in the east. There it joins Trail #10.

Continuing south on the Muir Trail, you pass a good campsite at the ford of Wright Creek (difficult in early season). Then your sandy trail ascends to a forested flat about ½ mile long, with a rather dense growth of lodgepole and foxtail pine. At the end of this flat is a photographer's overlook, where excellent pictures may be taken of the Great Western Divide. Then the trail descends steadily to Wallace Creek and a junction with the High Sierra Trail arriving from Giant Forest.

There are fair campsites near the ford (highly difficult in early season). Then the trail switchbacks steeply ½ mile up the south wall of Wallace Creek canyon over rocky going, lightly forested by lodgepole, whitebark and foxtail pine. The ascent becomes less steep where you ford an unnamed tributary and climb for another ⅓ mile. Then your route rounds the ridge up which you have been climbing, and passes above a pretty little lake in a meadow. Continuing your gentle climb on mostly sandy trail, you ford another runoff stream and enter a foxtail forest on a rocky hillside. From here, views to the north are good of Mt. Ericsson, Tawny Point, Junction Peak, Mt. Tyndall, Mt. Versteeg, Mt. Williamson, and Mt. Barnard.

Leveling off, the sandy trail winds below the huge boulders of a glacial moraine on the northwest slope of Mt. Young. From here you make a gentle traverse up to a saddle where the topo map says "BM 10964," and there is a bench mark at that elevation. From the saddle, a simple descent brings you through a sloping meadow, then a foxtail-pine forest, and then the gravelly slope called "Sandy Meadow" on the topo map. Where you cross little runoff streams, you may pause, dazzled by the intense yellow fields of groundsel and monkey flowers. From the second major ford beyond the saddle, you ascend for several hundred feet to an almost level trail section on a boulder-strewn slope dotted with foxtail pines. Because of their leaning tips and narrow profiles, these pines could almost pass for mountain hemlocks. On an overcast day, this foxtail forest has an eerie, gloomy, otherworldly quality.

On this level section, you meet a junction where the Pacific Crest Trail continues south to Crabtree Meadow; you turn left (east). In a moment the broad back of Mt. Whitney comes into view, and you switchback down to a sandy flat where there is another often-gloomy foxtail forest. As you approach Whitney Creek, lodgepole pines replace foxtails and you come to a junction with another trail to Crabtree Meadow. There is a summer ranger

Great Western Divide from lip of Wallace Creek ford

station on a spur trail branching off this trail. Along your trail and across the creek, near the ranger station (emergency services perhaps available) are some good campsites. During the busy season in late July and August, one may find more secluded camping at Upper Crabtree Meadow (½ mile south of the ranger station) or Lower Crabtree Meadow (1 mile south).

The Muir Trail stays high on the north bank as it ascends the narrowing canyon of Whitney Creek under a sparse forest cover of lodgepole and foxtail pine. In a meadow where two streams flow together, about ½ mile from the junction with the trail to Crabtree Meadow and the ranger station, are the last campsites below treeline. Ahead, Timberline Lake, just inside the Mt. Whitney Zone, though somewhat wooded, is closed to camping. It is, however, a fine spot for a rest stop, and the bulk of Mt. Whitney mirrored in the lake is quite photogenic.

From Timberline Lake you climb rather stiffly, veering away from Whitney Creek and leaving timber behind. The trail stays well above Guitar Lake, crossing an inlet coming from Arctic Lake. Guitar Lake is a popular but overused camping area. Now you veer southward, close under the mighty backside of Mt. Whitney, with excellent views of the avalanche-scarred north face of Mt. Hitchcock. The avalanche chutes there end partway down the face; their lower portions were smoothed off by the passage of the most recent glacier, and have not had time to redevelop since then.

Near a meadowy lakelet the climb steepens; then it levels off momentarily, and you can more or less catch your breath for the final assault on the 1500 vertical feet of switchbacks. On this climb, large yellow flowers called hulsea, or alpine gold, have anchored themselves in the most unlikely-looking places. The population pressure on this trail is evidenced by the frequent bedsites constructed in the granite wall, especially near switchbacks.

At 13,500′ you meet the Mt. Whitney Trail, coming up from Whitney Portal on the east side. Here your route, the John Muir Trail, turns left and begins the last two slogging miles to the summit of Mt. Whitney. As you wind among the large blocks of talus, you often have views, through notch-windows, of Owens Valley, 10,000′ below in the east. Closer below are the heads of barren glacial cirques, most of them containing brilliant turquoise lakes.

Finally, you see ahead on an almost level plateau a small cabin near the summit, and with a well-earned feeling of accomplishment you take the last few steps to the highest point in the "lower 48" states. The view from here is not indescribable — it has been described many times — but the authors prefer to let you see it with fresh eyes.

TRAIL #2

Shepherd Pass Trail (17 miles)

This long, steep trail is only for those in top condition whose reward will be a fast entrance into unpopulated high country. (Beginning in 1971, a policy of minimum trail maintenance was instituted. Downed trees may be removed and rock slides worked over a bit, but that's all.)

The trail begins at the mouth of Symmes Creek canyon and ascends on the south side of the creek through pinyon pine, sagebrush and, at streamside, alders, willows, and cottonwoods. The trail fords the creek four times (fill your container at the fourth), passing clumps of early and mid-season columbines. Beyond the fourth crossing the trail begins a long, gruelling series of rocky switchbacks that climb over 2000 feet to a saddle between Shepherd and Symmes creeks. Around 8000′ red fir and then silver pine* form a moderate forest cover and the entire hot slope is dotted with sagebrush, mountain mahogany, and cream bush.

From the saddle at the head of this slope, the great peak you see to the south is Mt. Williamson, second highest in California — though, surprisingly, it is not on the Sierra crest. The steep, deep gash that contains Shepherd Creek falls away at your feet, and it is an impressive introduction to the immense canyons of the eastern escarpment. From this viewpoint the sandy trail descends moderately over two small ridges high above Shepherd Creek before dropping 500′ down to a dry creek bed. From here the sunny trail climbs through a burned forest of pinyon pine to arrive at the only year-round water between Symmes Creek and Anvil Camp. Beyond this very welcome water the trail climbs to Mahogany Flat, where there is a poor campsite. At the upper end of this "flat" the trail begins a set of long, brushy switchbacks to gain the elevation of the creek's cascade visible to the southwest.

---

*Some people know the silver pine as the *western white pine.*

Mt. Williamson

As the route crosses a large talus slope, the environment changes dramatically within a few hundred feet. The trail thus far has been largely on decomposed granite, with the vegetation generally sparse and desertlike. But as the trail reaches Anvil Camp (10,000′) experienced Sierra travelers suddenly realizes that they are in the *High* Sierra: there is duff, a burbling stream, a campsite, willows, grass, and young lodgepole pines. Only hikers in the best of shape will choose to go over the pass the first day, and not camp here.

From Anvil Camp the trail ascends moderately up rocky slopes on the south side of Shepherd Creek. Your route crosses the area labeled "The Pothole" on the topo map, and ascends among large boulders to the giant declivity, below the pass, for which that label should have been reserved: a gargantuan jumble of great jagged rocks weathered out of the headwall of the cirque. The last 500′ ascent to Shepherd Pass (12,050′) is via switchbacks up a steep scree slope, which often has patches of snow into August.

(A cross-country route to Mt. Williamson basin begins at the pass. This basin, between Mt. Tyndall and Mt.

Williamson, is indeed a place to get away from it all. The route strikes out southeast to a saddle northeast of Tyndall and drops down to a lake at 12,200′, above treeline. The lake to the east of this one has good fishing for rainbow, and some beautiful falls below its outlet, but the route to this lake is quite circuitous, around to the cliffs east of it and then carefully down the steep talus.)

At the summit your route enters Sequoia National Park and begins a descent down a broad, boulder-strewn field to alpine meadows and scattered stands of foxtail pine. Immediately to the south is the northern flank of Mt. Tyndall, northernmost of the "Whitney group" of 14,000′ peaks. The sky along this crest is a marvelous blue on clear days, and it is fitting that John Tyndall, the English scientist for whom Mt. Tyndall was named, is the man who discovered why the sky is blue! He discovered the scattering of light by particles in the air, noting that the light waves of shortest wave length — the blue end of the spectrum — are scattered the most.

(A good cross-country route to the Wright Lakes leaves your trail at the 11,600′ level. This route traverses southwest to the saddle between Peak 13540 and Peak 12345, and then goes down the east wall of the cirque that lies south of the saddle. The lake basin is described in Trail #1.)

Your route continues down beside Tyndall Creek, through a vast, boulder-strewn, sloping meadow, the 13,000′ peaks of the Great Western Divide filling the western horizon. There are trails on both sides of the creek, but the one on the north side is more apparent.

After joining the Muir Trail, you ford Tyndall Creek and stroll south for a few hundred yards, past many heavily used campsites. Then you veer right onto the Tyndall Creek Trail and enter a mile-long meadow of uneven width. Soon you pass a patrol cabin and ford the creek. It is wet going around here except in late season, but the wildflowers don't complain — they thrive: aster, buttercup, shooting star, little elephant's head, western wallflower, and much lupine. Fair-to-good campsites may be found on both sides of the ford.

At the end of the meadow you pass a sheepherder's sod-roofed cabin that could provide shelter, and enter moderate-to-dense lodgepole forest cover. The under-footing varies from rock to duff as your route veers right and tops a gentle rise, arriving at the brink of steep-walled Kern River canyon. Views across the canyon to the Great Western Divide are excellent. From this viewpoint the trail descends steeply via a long series of switchbacks that lead 1200 vertical feet down to the aspen-clad banks of the young Kern River, where you meet Trail #3.

TRAIL #3
Kern River-Harrison Pass Trail (22.0 miles)

This long northbound trail leads from the southern border of the Mt. Kaweah 7.5′ topo map almost to the northern, ending with a difficult off-trail crossing of the Kings-Kern Divide. The trail ascends gently, sometimes a bit stiffly, beside the Kern River, heading almost due north. The **U**-shaped trough of the Kern River, called the Kern Trench, is remarkably straight for about 25 miles as it traces the Kern Canyon fault. The fault, a zone of structural weakness in the Sierra batholith, is more susceptible to erosion than the surrounding rock, and this deep canyon has been carved by both glacial and stream action. Three times the glacier advanced down the canyon, shearing off spurs created by stream erosion and leaving some tributary valleys hanging above the main valley. The glacier also scooped and plucked at the bedrock, creating basins in the granite which became lakes when the glacier melted and retreated.

The walls of this deep canyon, from 2000′ to 5000′ high, are quite spectacular, and a number of streams cascade and fall down these walls. (The fords of the streams draining Guyot Flat, Whitney Creek, and Wallace Creek can be difficult in early season.) The river is the home of hybrid trout whose origins have been variously interpreted, but whatever their origins, they taste fine, and they are not too hard to catch.

Six miles up the trail you come to a Junction Meadow. (Trail #5 starts at another Junction Meadow.) Here a park-like grove of stalwart Jeffrey pines provides a noble setting for a number of campsites. Beyond this meadow the trail ascends more steeply, up a hillside where the forest cover is mainly aspen with some pines — not dense enough to cut off the excellent view down the canyon. After 1 mile and 800 vertical feet, the sweating hiker appreciates it when the trail begins to level off, roughly at the junction where the High Sierra Trail to Mt. Whitney turns east.

Beginning one mile up the canyon from here, there are several good campsites along the river, where firewood is ample and fishing is good for rainbow.

Once past the campsites, the trail ascends less steeply, and soon it reaches the ford of Tyndall Creek (difficult in early season). Beyond the ford, the trail becomes sandier and drier, and the red fir and aspen gradually disappear, leaving a forest cover of lodgepole and some foxtail that is sparse on the hillsides and moderate on the river terraces. There are numerous campsites along this stretch of trail, including a packer campsite ½ mile beyond the Tyndall Creek Trail.

After passing the hard-to-spot Tyndall Creek Trail, your route becomes more exposed, with considerable sagebrush. The trail fords the outlet stream of Lake 11440 and soon comes to a dell thick with lodgepole trunks. The wildflower display in this large dell is dominated by yellow groundsel, but includes also orange tiger lilies, purple swamp onion, and red columbine. Above the dell, the trail

The only trouble with your time is that the future is not what it used to be.

— Paul Valery

Upper Kern landscape

ascends through a bank of shield fern, Queen Anne's lace, and brush chinquapin. Then, through a sparse lodgepole cover, your rocky trail ascends 600′ up granite slabs to the upper Kern Plateau. The trail then levels off and soon passes the junction with the Milestone Basin Trail.

Two hundred yards farther on you come to an unnamed lake at 10,700′, where a trail to Shepherd Pass branches right. Fishing and camping are good at this crossroads lake, but for solitude and sweeping beauty, the intrepid hiker will continue on to higher lakes.

A short half mile up the river, your route, now near treeline, passes another lake and veers eastward, climbing moderately under a sparse forest cover of lodgepole and whitebark pines. (At the 11,000′ contour the adventurous backpacker may turn north and curve west around the medium-large lake with three bays on its north side, bound for the high lakes between Table Mountain and Mt. Jordan. It would be hard to find a more remote part of the United States or a finer alpine setting for fishing and for absorbing the unsurpassed views in this upper Kern basin. Little pockets of timber along the creek offer some storm protection.)

Continue upward on the indistinct, ducked "trail" in the lake-dotted super-cirque under the Kings-Kern Divide, welcoming the need to pause for breath, as it allows you to look back at the superlative view to the south. Beyond three medium-sized lakes, the trail veers eastward and climbs somewhat steeply to a trail junction beside a little lake perched on a hilltop. It is easy to get carried away about this upper Kern country, but this little lake has to be called a jewel, with its preternaturally blue water rimmed along one side by snow the whole summer long, and its bordering clumps of fragile, fragrant, blue polemonium, the favorite flower of many mountaineers.

At the junction you take the signed trail to Lake South America, and very soon arrive at the shallow outlet. Your route, no longer a trail but marked only by ducks, continues north up a gentle slope above treeline. One may lose the ducks from time to time, but more appear as one simply heads for the low point on the divide ahead. All routes in this broad valley are good routes. Near the divide, a trail of use becomes evident again as it climbs eastward to reach the crest east of the lowest point on the saddle. Perhaps a cairn here marks the proper crossing of Harrison Pass. Views from the pass to the north are interrupted by the bulk of Deerhorn Mountain rising athwart your line of sight, but to the left of it in the distance you can see Mt. Goddard, and to the right, Middle Palisade. In the south, landmarks include Mt. Kaweah, Kaweah Peaks Ridge, Milestone Mountain, and Mt. Guyot.

The descent down the north side of the pass is difficult, and should be attempted only by experienced mountaineers, as it may require rope. In some years the snow lies deep on this steep slope all summer long. It is hard to believe that Robert Pike took horses and donkeys northward over the pass (then called Madary's Pass) on July 4, 1901, or that Force Parker took horses southward over the pass two years later. Pike wrote afterward, "On looking down it, you were strongly impressed with the fact that places called 'passes' differ widely in character." As for Parker, his party reached the top at 4 A.M. In any event, the route is Class 2, if a rather high 2. Keep to the east side of the chute for the first 75′ from the crest, then move to its center. Carefully pick your way downward, toward the first lake visible on the cirque floor. Cross its outlet and veer west to ford the stream connecting the second and third lakes in the cirque. From here the sometimes ducked route ascends a few hundred feet and then drops to the outlet of the third lake, passing close under the buff-and-tan granite cliffs of soaring Ericsson Crags. In the canyon below the third lake you encounter timber, and also achieve your first view of Mt. Brewer, due west across the canyon of East Creek. The route then levels off briefly in a meadow and fords the crystal stream to the north side. The white color of the trumpet-shaped flowers of alpine gentian in this meadow tells you that you are still quite high; blue gentians lie below. After passing several lovely tarns not shown on the topo map, the ducked and sometimes blazed route easily crosses a little divide on a southbound course and traverses down to Golden Lake (not named on the topo map), where there is one excellent campsite and wood is plentiful. From the lake you have a direct view of Lucy's Foot Pass, on the Kings-Kern Divide. This pass is Class 3 in places and it is not advised for ordinary backpacking or inexperienced mountaineers. Due to all the loose "garbage" on the north side, the best passage is south-to-north.

From Golden Lake the route (not a trail) has a short level segment and then it descends steeply on a rocky-dusty route to the East Creek Trail, meeting it at an unsigned junction 50 yards north of a talus rock slide.

The richest values of wilderness lie not in the days of Daniel Boone, nor even in the present, but rather in the future.

— Aldo Leopold

TRAIL #4

Junction Pass Trail to Center Basin (7.5 miles)

This unmaintained trail, once part of the Muir Trail — now barely a route — provides access from the southeast to Center Basin, a beautiful, high basin off the beaten track and little visited. The route is here described south-to-north, as the shortest access route to Center Basin, but the going is better north-to-south. Access from the north is via Kearsarge Pass. Don't try this route unless you are an experienced mountaineer.

The Junction Pass Trail leaves the Shepherd Pass Trail about one mile uphill from Anvil Camp, near the confluence of two tributaries of Shepherd Creek. The trail is very hard to follow, if not impossible. Before Forester Pass was completed in 1932, the southbound John Muir Trail ascended into Center Basin, crossed Junction Pass, dropped down to the Shepherd Pass Trail, and followed it over the Sierra crest to the confluence of the main forks of Tyndall Creek. Following this route, it did not cross but bypassed the Kings-Kern Divide.

Leaving the Shepherd Pass Trail, you soon pass a lovely subalpine meadow, and then turn westward up a steep slope near treeline. You may, with luck, find the old trail at about 11,600′, well above treeline, about 300 yards east of the big bend in the unnamed tributary on the topo map. From here you proceed west near the stream for more than a mile along the north slope of the tributary valley. Then, at about 12,500′ elevation, your route veers northward and climbs very steeply up a talus slope to the flat saddle northeast of pyramidal Junction Peak. (If you miss this northward turn, your climb up the talus will be very difficult, and at the head of the canyon it will be impossible.) Views north from the pass (13,200′) are awe-inspiring, and the sheer east face of Mt. Tyndall in the southeast is a lesson in the process of cirque formation.

Tyndall, Whitney from south of Forester Pass

From the pass your route swings west to a ridge that affords a northward way down along a rocky traverse to upper Center Basin. Here, a scant airline mile from the Muir Trail, solitary splendid grandeur rewards the dedicated hiker and it is only with some regret that you head on down the basin toward "civilization." You may tarry to climb Center Peak via the east slope or camp on Lake 11776, where campsites are good. Approaching the map-indicated Center Basin, the trail levels off and threads a series of alpine, flower-clouded meadows. Golden Bear Lake, in the heart of the basin close under Center Peak, offers some fair campsites on its timbered northern shore. From the lake your trail loops north around several wide places in the creek, and then makes a steepening descent into increasingly dense timber cover. After fording an unnamed tributary amid lush flower gardens, you switchback down to join the Muir Trail at 10,500′ beside Bubbs Creek.

TRAIL #5

Junction Meadow on Bubbs Creek to Lake Reflection (5.0 miles)

This spur trail leads away from the heavily traveled Rae Lakes Loop to a famous lake under the Kings-Kern Divide, a base-camp area for many cross-country adventures.

Your trail starts at a Junction Meadow. (Trail #3 passes through another Junction Meadow.) The trail turns south from the Bubbs Creek Trail and crosses the creek on a log bridge. Immediately, it begins a switchbacking ascent up a fairly steep slope, sometimes in the forest shade and sometimes in open, sunny enclaves. The trail leaves streamside under red firs but these gradually disappear as you ascend the dry slope, and lodgepole and silver pine become more common.

As the trail ascends through broken granite, brush, and grass, one should pause to look back at the deeply fluted south face of Mt. Bago across Bubbs Creek canyon. The grade eases somewhat before you cross East Creek via a log-and-plank bridge. The trail here, a section built in 1979, stays close to the east bank of tumultuous East Creek. The grade increases before the trail enters a foxtail-pine forest and switchbacks up the east canyon wall. The trail then fords the fern-lined outlet from Lake 11322, where the hiker can pleasure his eyes with the sight of yellow mimulus and purple monkshood. Beyond this ford the trail tops a slight rise, and you can see East Lake through the trees ahead.

East Lake is a beautiful sight; good campsites line the north and south shores. This lake is the traditional base for climbing Mt. Brewer, via the east ridge. From the lake's inlet your trail climbs steadily up willowed meadows, their grassy slopes decorated with flowers of pennyroyal, monkey flower, Indian paintbrush, and yarrow milfoil. Between East Lake and Lake Reflection you have to cope with a lot of avalanche debris.

About a mile from East Lake you pass the unsigned "junction" with the route to Harrison Pass (Trail #3). This is just before a 50-yard-wide talus rock slide, which you must boulder-hop more or less following a line of ducks. After the rock slide, you pass a number of good campsites beside fish-filled East Creek. The last ½ mile of ascent to Lake Reflection is on a gentle grade through turfy meadow and willow thicket.

There is a large, good campsite beside the lakelet below Reflection, but the best campsites are on the west side of the northernmost bay of the lake. The mirroring reflections from which the lake presumably takes its name are best seen from the granite "beach" here. However, the lake is the scene of another kind of reflection, which might possibly have led to the naming. When a stormy late-afternoon wind is blowing through the gap west of the lake, one may climb the northwestern shore and witness a remarkable interplay of air, water, and light. A gust of wind (heard before it is seen) creates ripples that move across the lake. The same gust is reflected off the steep wall on the other side of the lake, and it then creates other ripples moving in a different direction. The low sun illuminates the different groups of advancing ripples at different angles, producing a delightful variety of blues, greens, and silvery whites. In addition, the different ripples interfere with each other, producing interference patterns just like the ones studied in optics and hydrodynamics, and these patterns in turn are subjects for magnificent light reflections. Very few lakes have the proper size and setting for these phenomena. Lake Reflection does.

This lake is a traditional base camp for climbing the nearby peaks of the Kings-Kern and the Great Western divides. A trail that ascends southward from the outlet turns into a ducked route over Millys Foot Pass (Class 3) and an old trail over Longley Pass can be fairly well followed if one looks for blazes and ducks, beginning on the slopes west of the inlet.

TRAIL #6

From the Muir Trail to the Kern River Trail (3.5 miles)

This trail connects the Muir Trail with the Kern River Trail, providing a link in the access to Milestone Basin and other remote country west of the river. It begins ⅛ mile north of the Tyndall Creek ford on the Muir Trail.

Following the trail signed MILESTONE CREEK and LAKE SOUTH AMERICA, this route heads west on nearly level footing across flower-dotted alpine fell fields. After ½ mile, you take the left fork at a **Y**, leaving the Lake South America Trail. Views in this upper Kern Basin are at all times panoramic and the traveler will mentally record pictures of the skyline that will not soon fade. At the outlet of Lake 11440 the angler can jog northward a short way to sample the good fishing for golden trout. Equally, the knapsacker who likes to camp alone may follow the outlet for 0.3 mile down to a good campsite beside a grove of foxtail pines near the stream.

From the easy ford of this outlet stream, your trail skirts the north side of a small lake, and makes a short rocky climb to a ridge where the descent to the Kern River begins. From the ridge the traveler has closer views of Mt. Jordan, Thunder Mountain, Milestone Mountain, Midway Mountain, Kern Ridge, and Red Spur. The trail descends moderately through rocky and meadowy sections with a moderate cover of high-altitude pines and arrives at a picturebook lake (you probably have the books) that is fast turning to meadow, geologically speaking. One might regret that all these high lakes are doomed, but you may enjoy the blend of meadows and lakes that now exist.

After climbing slightly from this lake, your route makes a last, steep, dusty descent to the Kern River, where it emerges at an unnamed lake at 10,700′ elevation (good fishing for golden and rainbow-golden hybrids to 10″; good camping).

Milestone Mountain

If a person lost would conclude that after all he is not lost, he is not beside himself, but standing in his own old shoes on the very spot where he is, and that for the time being he will live there; but the places that have known him, they are lost . . . how much anxiety and danger would vanish.

— Henry David Thoreau

TRAIL #7

From Trail #6 to Trail #3 (2.0 miles)

This trail segment connects Trail #6 with Lake South America, where it meets Trail #3. It provides a shorter way to Harrison Pass from Whitney Portal or Symmes Creek Roadend.

From the Milestone Creek/Lake South America Trail junction you ascend gently northward up the east side of a long, boulder-strewn meadow. Two shallow, unnamed lakes in the middle of this meadow have variable borders: in early and mid-season, only a detour will prevent wet feet. The silent hiker may be able to approach very close to some of the marmots and pikas which claim this rocky upland as their home. Views of the high peaks around Mt. Whitney improve gradually, and then more rapidly as the trail makes a fairly steep 500′ ascent to a saddle that leads to the large cirque basin at the head of the Kern River. About ⅓ mile beyond the saddle, beside one of the prettiest tarns in this entire area, this route meets Trail #3.

TRAIL #8

Milestone Basin Trail (3.0 miles)

This spur trail leads from the Kern River Trail (Trail #3) into the high, beautiful, remote recesses of Milestone Basin.

The unsigned junction where the Milestone Trail begins is located about 200 yards down the Kern River Trail from the unnamed lake at 10,700′ elevation. After fording the river (difficult in early season), the trail continues around to meet Milestone Creek. A campsite here is very unpleasant during the height of the mosquito season. Your route then veers west up a rocky slope away from the creek. After another ½ mile it rejoins the creek at a bench where there is a good campsite beside a waterfall. Wood is ample, and fishing in Milestone Creek is good. Views are excellent across the plateau to Mt. Whitney, as they are from so many points in this magnificent high country.

Those who wish to camp as high as possible in the Milestone Basin may climb to the high lake (11,900′) that lies just to the right of Midway Mountain. A trail, shown on the topo map, located beside Milestone Creek above the confluence of the north fork does not exist. Instead, you should follow the ducked route that turns right up the north fork, passes west through a defile, skirts a small, barren lake and traverses up to the high lake, where fishing is good for golden trout. There are fair campsites below this lake on the outlet stream.

TRAIL #9

Junction Meadow to Colby Pass (8.5 miles)

This trail leads upward from the Kern River to Colby Pass, a primitive route over the Great Western Divide, on the way to Horse Corral Meadow or Cedar Grove.

This route is unmaintained and impassable to stock, but a backpacker with any experience will have little trouble staying on the route. Soon after the ford of the Kern River (very difficult in early season) the trail begins the steep ascent up the Kern Canyon wall to the hanging valley above. Veering away from the Kern-Kaweah River, it ascends to the north side of a granite knob, or spine, and passes through what has been called "Kern-Kaweah Pass." This difficult climb is repaid by the delightful valley above it, one of the finest in the Sierra. From the "pass" the trail descends very steeply to Rockslide Lake, with its crystal-clear, emerald-green water. (A difficult but thrilling cross-country route to the Chagoopa Plateau goes up the west side of Picket Creek from Rockslide Lake, crossing over to the next creek to the south — unnamed — after climbing out of Kern-Kaweah Canyon. It crosses the divide just east of Mt. Kaweah.)

Just beyond Rockslide Lake the canyon widens into a kind of granite amphitheater, from which you make a steady ascent through a sparse-to-moderate lodgepole cover as the trail threads the deep canyon lying between Kern Point and Picket Guard Peak. One more steep ascent is required to reach the bowl that contains Gallats Lake, really a large meander in a large, wet meadow. Fair campsites are here, but the traveler will prefer those about one mile ahead, where the trail turns away from the stream toward Colby Pass.

Leaving the Kern-Kaweah behind, the trail ascends steeply, and quickly transcends the sparse cover of lodgepole pine. This steep climb offers magnificent views back into the headwaters of the Kern-Kaweah watershed and the backgrounding Kaweah Peaks Ridge. Just north of these distinctive summits rise the pyramidal heights of Triple Divide Peak, which trifurcates the drainages of the Kern, Kings, and Kaweah rivers. The steepness of the ascent is relieved briefly as you cross the tributaries draining Milestone Bowl. Then, by a faint and unreliably ducked trail, the route resumes its steep climb to Colby Pass (12,000′). Here one has grand views down Cloud Canyon and of Glacier Ridge and the cockscomblike sentinels atop Whaleback Ridge.

TRAIL #10

Kern River to Wallace Lake (9.0 miles)

This trail first connects the Kern River Trail with the John Muir Trail, and then penetrates the Sierra crest to a high lake famous for its fishing. It is no longer being maintained.

From a trail junction about one mile north of Junction Meadow, your route makes a long, hot, moderately steep traverse toward Wallace Creek canyon. The sparse forest cover of Jeffrey pine and mountain juniper leaves the afternoon hiker mostly exposed, and you should carry water. From this trail, views are excellent down the great Kern River Trench, and photographers will often stop here to select exposures. The granite slopes are well covered by a number of flowering bushes, including manzanita, creambush, hollyleaf redberry, mountain mahogany, and Sierra chinquapin. Shortly after the trail circles left around a ridge, you come upon a single foxtail pine, which will be a first sighting to those who have entered this area from Giant Forest. Where the trail nears Wallace Creek in its steep-sided canyon, the forest turns to mixed lodgepole and foxtail, moderately spaced. A fair campsite may be found below the trail, near where a bench mark at 9700′ is cemented into a rock on the south side of the trail.

From this plaque, the route makes a moderate ascent through sparse lodgepole to a ford of Wright Creek, then a gentler ascent through denser forest. Fair to good campsites are on both sides of the trail here, and the forest scene is considerably brightened by the many hues of fireweed, paintbrush, arnica, sulfur flower, wild buckwheat, pennyroyal, mountain pride, and creambush. One more short ascent, on an exposed rocky slope, brings you to a sandy, almost level trail section, and this easy footing lasts for a few hundred yards, to a junction with the John Muir Trail. There are fair campsites, with scarce wood, south of Wallace Creek near the junction.

Continuing up the north side of the creek, your trail (no longer maintained) ascends gently under a cover of sparse-to-moderate lodgepole pine. The shaded forest floor is sprinkled with western wallflower, penstemon, groundsel, yarrow milfoil, and Labrador tea. Contrary to the topo-map trail, at the meadow where the outlet of Wales Lake joins Wallace Creek the trail fords Wallace Creek and then fords the tributary, staying on the south side of Wallace Creek. Here the ascent becomes moderate for a short distance, then reverts to a gentler grade. This route up Wallace Creek canyon is sometimes indistinct and sometimes confused by multiple trail sections and inadequate ducking. Careful negotiation of the indistinct sections will bring one to the fair campsites at treeline (11,400′), about ½ mile below Wallace Lake which lies in a giant bowl at the foot of the arête that connects Mt. Barnard with Tunnebora Peak. Wallace Lake is a base for the Class 1 climb of Mt. Barnard. Fishing in Wallace Lake is good for golden; the same is true of Wales Lake (though the fish are smaller), reached by cross-country southwest from the inlet of Wallace Lake.

TRAIL #11

Whitney Portal to the Muir Trail (8.5 miles)

This highly popular, crowded trail provides the one short way from a road to the highest summit in the "lower 48" states. If one is able to postpone one's trip until after Labor Day, it will not be crowded.

From just east of a small store (8361′) the route steadily climbs through a moderate forest cover of Jeffrey pine and red fir. After ½ mile the trail crosses North Fork Lone Pine Creek and shortly enters John Muir Wilderness. Soon the forest cover thins, and the slope is covered with a chaparral that includes mountain mahogany, Sierra chinquapin, and sagebrush. This steep slope can get very hot in midmorning, and the trip is best begun as early as possible. Breather stops on this trail provide a "Veed" view down the canyon framing the Alabama Hills.

Then the trail levels off somewhat through several willow-covered pockets having a modest forest cover of lodgepole and foxtail pines, and passes fields of corn lilies, delphinium, tall lupine, and swamp whiteheads. In 1½ miles you approach a ford of Lone Pine Creek, which will be your first water source in late season. Beyond the log ford is a junction with a spur trail to nearby, visible Lone Pine Lake. Turning up a barren wash, you enter the Mt. Whitney Zone, then switchback up another rocky slope under a moderate lodgepole cover to Outpost Camp, a willow-covered meadow that was once a lake. Packers once used this meadow as the last grazing area on the ascent to the Sierra crest, and a packer's wife ran an overnight camp where food and tent-lodging could be bought.

Your trail veers away from the waterfall that tumbles down into Outpost Camp from the southwest, fords Lone Pine Creek and begins a short series of switchbacks beside the cascading creek, past blossoming creambush, Indian paintbrush, Sierra chinquapin, mountain pride, currant, pennyroyal, fireweed, and groundsel. Then the trail boulder-hops the creek and arrives at Mirror Lake (10,640′), cradled in its cirque beneath the south face of Thor Peak. This cold lake has fair fishing for rainbow and brook, but camping is no longer allowed here. The Forest Service closed the lake to camping in 1972 after severe overuse had created a montane slum. Since then, the lakeshore has begun to recover, and after a great many years it may look something like it did when first discovered.

Leaving Mirror Lake, the trail ascends the south wall of the Mirror Lake cirque via switchbacks. At the top of the ascent the trail passes treeline, as a last foxtail pine and a broken, weathered, convoluted whitebark snag are seen, along with a few last willows. Soon Mt. Whitney comes into view, over Pinnacle Ridge. From here, the rocky trail ascends moderately alongside the gigantic boulders on the north side of South Fork Lone Pine Creek. In the cracks in the boulders you will find ivesia, cinquefoil, creambush, currant and much gooseberry, and looking across the canyon the cascading outlet of Consultation Lake is visible. Beside a ford of the stream are specimens of the moisture-loving shooting star. After ascending over some poured concrete steps — which unfortunately detract from the wilderness feel of this country — the trail arrives at the overused last campsites before the crest — Trail Camp (12,000′). Here beneath Wotans Throne is also the last reliable water in late season. There are numerous level campsites, but no fires are allowed.

As the trail begins the one hundred or so switchbacks to Trail Crest (the name of the pass), Mt. Whitney is occluded by a sharp spire, and Mt. Russell, farther north, comes into view. This rocky, barren talus slope is not *entirely* barren, for one may see a dozen species of flowering plants, climaxed by the multiflowered, blue "sky pilot." The building of this trail section involved much blasting with dynamite, and the natural fracture planes of the granite are evident in the blasted slabs. Finally the 1700′ ascent from Trail Camp ends at Trail Crest (13,620′), and the hiker suddenly has vistas of a great part of Sequoia

National Park to the west, including the entire Great Western Divide. To the east, far below, are Consultation Lake and several smaller, unnamed lakes, lying close under the Whitney crest. These lakes may not be free of ice the whole summer. From Trail Crest the route descends for a short 0.1 mile to the junction with the John Muir Trail, which terminates atop Mt. Whitney (see Trail #1).

TRAIL #12

Crabtree Meadow to Rock Creek (24 miles)

This loop trip, partly cross-country, tours the remote, grand high country in the southeast corner of the quadrangle.

In Upper Crabtree Meadow, about ½ mile south of the Crabtree Ranger Station, a trail ascends to Crabtree Lakes. First the route takes you along the south side of the meadow, then it ascends moderately through a lodgepole forest, on a slope above Crabtree Creek. At the first Crabtree Lake is a packer campsite, but in comparison to campsites on the Muir Trail it is little used. Your route ascends moderately over boulders to the largest Crabtree Lake, with a spectacular wall just south of it, culminating in Mt. Chamberlain. As you approach this lake, the trail ends on granite slabs and you keep well to the north on these slabs. Beyond the lake, staying on the north side of the creek, sometimes a slight distance from it, you arrive at the uppermost lake in this watershed.

From this lake you can see an obvious saddle to the southeast, and you reach it via a short, steep scramble, over talus. From this cairned saddle, the view west of Mt. Kaweah and Kaweah Peaks Ridge is excellent, and you have closer views of Mt. McAdie, Mt. Newcomb, and the flat-topped Major General, as well as the lakes on your path of descent. The first lake, Lake 12125, is utterly hemmed in by granite, and has no campsites. Making

Lateral moraine near Crabtree Meadow

your way down the drainage southeastward, you circle Sky Blue Lake on its east side. Camping is possible here in several level, grassy spots, but there is no wood until you reach the next basin down the stream. This rocky basin provides the viewpoint for seeing "The Miter" as a miter.

The high, jagged, fractured, cliffed granite formations in this country are a great attraction for climbers, and some of them can be climbed without expertise (see the chapter "Climbers").

Where the canyon narrows and the descent steepens, the tree cover increases to moderate, and foxtail joins lodgepole. Eventually you begin to see a trail on the west side of the creek, well used and sometimes blazed. This trail threads a small, wet meadow and then becomes indistinct as it nears the unnamed lake on Rock Creek. There are excellent campsites on the northwest side of this lake. A trail up the tributary to the east leads, in less than a mile, to a junction with the Army Pass Trail. This tributary descends from the Soldier Lakes (unnamed on the topo map, lying south of The Major General). Good campsites may be found on the east side of the lower lake.

Past the outlet, the trail descends steadily alongside the now-cascading stream. The dense green forest cover provides the shade that gooseberries prefer, and these thorny, edible plants are frequent in this trail section. After about 2 miles the trail fords Rock Creek in a meadow lush with many species of wildflowers in mid season; in another ¾ mile you meet and step onto the Pacific Crest Trail. This trail descends moderately through often-heavy lodgepole forest cover to the banks of Rock Creek, and soon reaches some large campsites.

Then, fording Rock Creek on a downed lodgepole, your route veers north and climbs steeply up the canyon wall. The grade lessens as you ford Guyot Creek (last water for over 4 miles) and then increases again as you climb around boulders to a forested saddle. From this saddle there is an excellent view of Red Spur, a newly barren hulk of reddish rock, on whose lake-dotted slopes one can spend days without seeing anybody. Then your route descends moderately to the large, sandy basin of Guyot Flat. Geologists estimate that the sand here is over 100′ deep, and the resulting drainage affords little opportunity for plant seeding or growth.

Beyond Guyot Flat the trail undulates under a moderate forest cover before dropping steeply into the Whitney Creek drainage. On this descent you have views eastward of Mt. Whitney, looking most unlike its aspect from Lone Pine: it is broad, flat-topped, domish, and avalanche-chuted. Shortly before you reach Whitney Creek a trail of use goes west down the canyon, to the Kern River Trail. At the creek ford is a good campsite, with good views and some wood. Up the creek 100 yards is another good

The maintenance of biological and mental health requires that technological societies provide in some form the biological freedom enjoyed by your Paleolithic ancestors.

— Rene Dubos

campsite, and farther on a packer campsite. From the trail junction in Upper Crabtree Meadow where this loop began, it is only a short ascent to the John Muir Trail near the Crabtree Ranger Station.

Travel Methods

THERE ARE THREE METHODS used to travel the trails described in this book. They are (1) on foot, either by dayhikes or with a backpack; (2) on horseback, with or without a pack string; or (3) on foot while leading a burro or a mule. Motorized vehicles are outlawed in Wilderness Areas and on trails in National Parks. The method one decides upon should take into account the purpose of the trip (fishing, nature study, photography, cross-country walking, etc.), grazing restrictions, personal condition (health, age), and length of time one plans to spend in the back country.

The most popular of the three is to go on foot with a backpack. The reasons given for this choice by backpackers are that they feel backpacking lets them get "closer to the country," and that backpacking is more economical. Travel on horseback is a second choice, employed by those who like the principle of long-term base camps, and/or those who are physically incapable of traveling long distances on foot. Those who lead burros, or "walking mules" are, by definition, in-betweeners. (Note: availability of burros and "walking mules" should be determined with packers before deciding upon this method.)

He who travels alone arrives alone.

— Lawrence Ferlinghetti

Backpackers

BECAUSE THE BACKPACKER CARRIES "his home on his back," he is free, within the limitations of stamina and food, to go as far as he likes. Two week back-country trips are not overly long excursions, if the backpacker plans his food and gear carefully. With caches or base-camp setups, he can extend his trip even longer. This prolonged duration is less a result of hardier backpackers being bred than of more and better light-weight equipment being manufactured.

Ever aware of the advantages of lightweight equipment and the increasing array of freeze-dried foods, the backpacker devotes his on-the-trail gab sessions to "shop talk." There is, in fact, a tendency to make a fetish of equipment, and "go-lighters" should constantly remind themselves of their purpose in going to wilderness. With this thought in mind, the editors have prepared the following list — an itemization of basics without a lengthy discussion of comparative differences in style.

To wear or carry in a readily accessible place

hat or cap
dark glasses
shirt
pants
belt
boots
socks
bandana
underwear
maps
compass
insect repellent
chapstick
first-aid kit
rain garment
flashlight
whistle
pencil and paper (for leaving notes)
Sierra cup
water bottle(s)
*fishing license
Wilderness Permit
waterproof matches
toilet paper
watch
knife
sunscreen
camera and film
spare change for phone
quick-energy food
water purifier

To carry in the pack

tent or tarp
sleeping bag
ground sheet
air mattress or foam pad
*pillowcase
extra shirt
extra pants
extra underwear
extra socks
jacket, sweater, or vest
*camp shoes or moccasins
gloves
knit cap or balaclava
extra bandanas
duct tape
sewing kit
*extra prescription glasses
extra flashlight batteries and bulb
braided nylon cord
collapsible plastic bucket
plastic bags — assorted
rubber bands
candle
towel
food
cooking gear
*grate
plastic bowl
spoon
*fishing tackle
*book
*camera equipment
*musical instrument
toothbrush
toothpaste or powder
comb or brush

*Optional

The way to travel the farthest in the shortest distance, is to go afoot.

— Henry David Thoreau

Packers

THOSE WHO PROVIDE rental stock and guides for back-country trips into the Sierra are called "packers." Packers do not make a practice of outfitting their customers beyond the requisite stock, saddles, and gearbags. Their usual service includes guiding, and the customer has the alternatives of having the stock and the wrangler/guide along for the duration of the trip, or asking for a "spot trip." The latter is an agreement between packer and guests that they and their gear will be transported to a designated campsite, and that the packer will return at a stipulated time to transport them back to the pack station.

Reservation arrangements for a packer's services should be made well in advance, and should include the following information in the initial correspondence:

1. How many persons will there be in your party?
2. Approximately what dates will you want to pack in and pack out?
3. To what lakes or to what area do you wish to pack?
4. If you have a route preference (perhaps described in this book) what is it?
5. Will you want the continuous hire of the packers and animals, or will you want a spot trip?
6. How many pounds do you estimate your pack load will be?

Prices for packers' services vary, and should be determined by correspondence with the individual packer.

Whether planning a trip on horseback or afoot, the basic clothing to be worn on the trail is the same. (See previous chapter).

Mts. Bradley and Keith from Forester Pass

Climbers

GOOD CLIMBING OPPORTUNITIES are plentiful in the Mt. Whitney region. There are 25 named peaks above 13,500′, and they all have impressive views, as do many of the lower peaks. Climbs are rated by their difficulty, beginning with Class 1 and going through Class 5. Class 1 routes are "walk ups" and Class 2 routes are easy scrambles. An unusually large proportion of the peaks in Mt. Whitney are either Class 1 or Class 2, and they are accessible to the average backpacker.

The following peaks have either Class 1 or Class 2 routes. (For details, see *Climbers Guide to the High Sierra*, listed in "Recommended Reading" on page 67.)

Mt. Barnard
Mt. Brewer
Mt. Bradley
Caltech Peak
Mt. Carillon
Center Peak
Mt. Chamberlain
Discovery Pinnacle
Mt. Ericsson
Mt. Genevra
Gregorys Monument
Mt. Guyot
Mt. Hale
Mt. Hitchcock
Mt. Irvine
Joe Devel Peak
Mt. Kaweah
Keeler Needle
Mt. Keith
Kern Point
The Major General
Mt. Mallory
Midway Mountain
Mt. Newcomb
Mt. Pickering
Picket Guard Peak
Red Spur
South Guard
Tawny Point
Thor Peak
Trojan Peak
Tunnabora Peak
Mt. Tyndall
University Peak
West Spur Peak
West Vidette
Mt. Whitney
Mt. Williamson
Wotans Throne
Mt. Young

Peak 13540 (1 mi. SW of Mt. Tyndall)
Peak 13030 (1 mi. S of Caltech Peak)
Peak 13285 (1.5 mi. NE of Mt. Kaweah)
Peak 13040± (0.5 mi. E of Shepherd Pass)

Recommended Reading

General and History

Austin, Mary. *Land of Little Rain.* New York: Viking Penguin, 1988.

Brewer, William H. *Up and Down California.* Berkeley: University of California Press, 1974.

Farquhar, Francis P. *History of the Sierra Nevada.* Berkeley: University of California Press, 1965.

Graydon, Don, ed. *Mountaineering, the Freedom of the Hills.* 4th edition. Seattle: The Mountaineers, 1992.

Gudde, Edwin G. *California Place Names.* Berkeley: University of California Press, 1969.

King, Clarence. *Mountaineering in the Sierra Nevada.* Books on Demand, 1971.

Roper, Steve. *Climbers Guide to the High Sierra.* San Francisco: Sierra Club, 1976.

Sierra Club. *Sierra Club Bulletins.* (Various volumes.) San Francisco: Sierra Club.

Storer, Tracy, and Usinger, Robert. *Sierra Nevada Natural History.* Berkeley: University of California Press, 1963.

Biology and Botany

Grater, Russell K., and Blaue, Tom A. *Discovering Sierra Mammals.* El Portal: Yosemite Association, 1978.

Hickman, James C. *The Jepson Manual: Higher Plants of California.* University of California Press, 1993.

Horn, Elizabeth L. *Sierra Nevada Wildflowers.* Missoula, MT: Mountain Press, 1998.

Munz, Philip. *California Mountain Wildflowers.* Berkeley: University of California Press, 1963.

Niehaus, Theodore F., and Ripper, Charles L. *A Field Guide to Pacific States Wildflowers.* Boston: Houghton Mifflin, 1981.

Peterson, P. Victor, and Peterson, P. Victor, Jr. *Native Trees of the Sierra Nevada.* Berkeley: University of California Press, 1975.

Peterson, Roger Tory. *A Field Guide to Western Birds.* Boston: Houghton Mifflin, 1990.

Sibley, David Allen. *National Audubon Society: The Sibley Guide to Birds.* New York: Knopf, 2000.

Watts, Tom. *Pacific Coast Tree Finder.* Berkeley: Nature Study Guilde, 1973.

Geology

Bateman, Paul C. *Plutonism in the Central Part of the Sierra Nevada Batholith, California.* Washington: U.S. Geological Survey, Professional Paper 1483, 1992.

Moore, James G. *Geologic Map of the Mount Whitney Quadrangle, Inyo and Tulare Counties, California.* Washington: U.S. Geological Survey, Map GQ-1545, 1991.

Wilderness Press publishes over 100 books and maps to the West and beyond. Here are a few that complement the Mt. Whitney area:

Backhurst, Paul, ed. *Backpacking California,* 2001.

Browning, Peter. *Place Names of the Sierra Nevada,* 1991.

Darvill, Jr., Fred. *Mountaineering Medicine,* 1998.

Morey, Kathy. *Hot Showers, Soft Beds, and Dayhikes in the Sierra,* 1996.

Schaffer, Jeffrey P. *et al. The Pacific Crest Trail, Vol. 1,* revised 1995.

Schaffer, Jeffrey P. *The Geomorphic Evolution of the Yosemite Valley and the Sierra Nevada Landscapes,* 1997.

Weeden, Norman. *A Sierra Nevada Flora,* revised 1996.

Winnett, Thomas, and Morey, Kathy. *Guide to the John Muir Trail,* revised 1998.

Winnett, Thomas, *et al. Sierra South,* 2001, 7th edition.

Winnett, Thomas, with Findling, Melanie. *Backpacking Basics,* 1994, 4th edition.

Trail Profiles

The trail profiles on the following pages will help hikers plan their trips. With a pack of about ⅕ your body weight, you can expect to cover two horizontal miles per hour. Add one hour for each 1000 feet of elevation gain. Though, if you are going 12 miles, and the total of all the "ups" is 1500 feet, you can expect to be walking for about: 6 hours + 1.5 hours = 7½ hours. This includes "normal" rest stops.

For downhill walking, use the figure of two miles per hour except where the trail is steep. A steep section will require an extra hour for 2000 feet of descent.

If you are walking without a pack, or you are in really excellent condition, you can do better — perhaps up to 50% better.

If you are walking cross-country, it may take you all day to go even two miles. There is wide variation, depending on the slope, the footing, the ground cover, and your condition.

The symbol **S** means "ford," but there may be no running water there in the late summer. Since bridges require no fording, they are not shown.

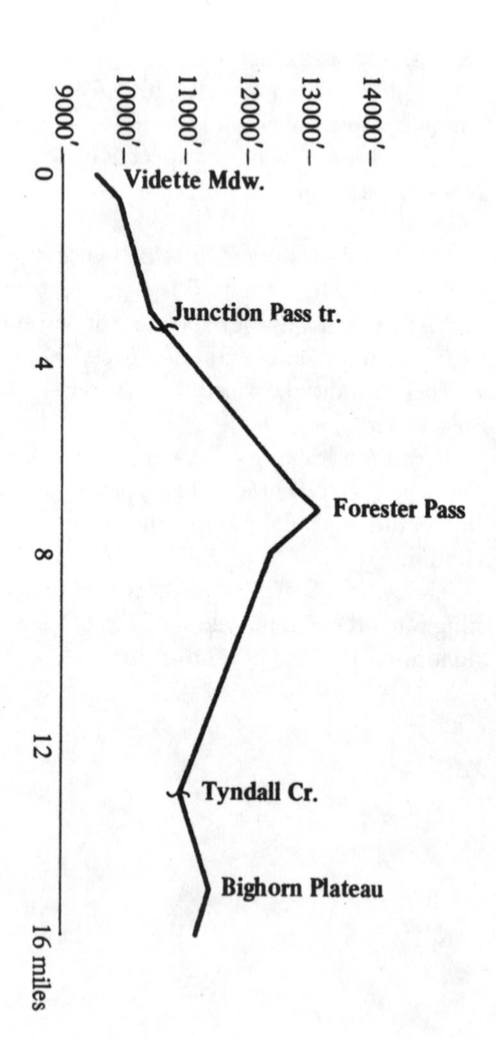
14000′
13000′
12000′
11000′
10000′
9000′
0
4
8
12
16 miles
Vidette Mdw.
Junction Pass tr.
Forester Pass
Tyndall Cr.
Bighorn Plateau
Trail # 1

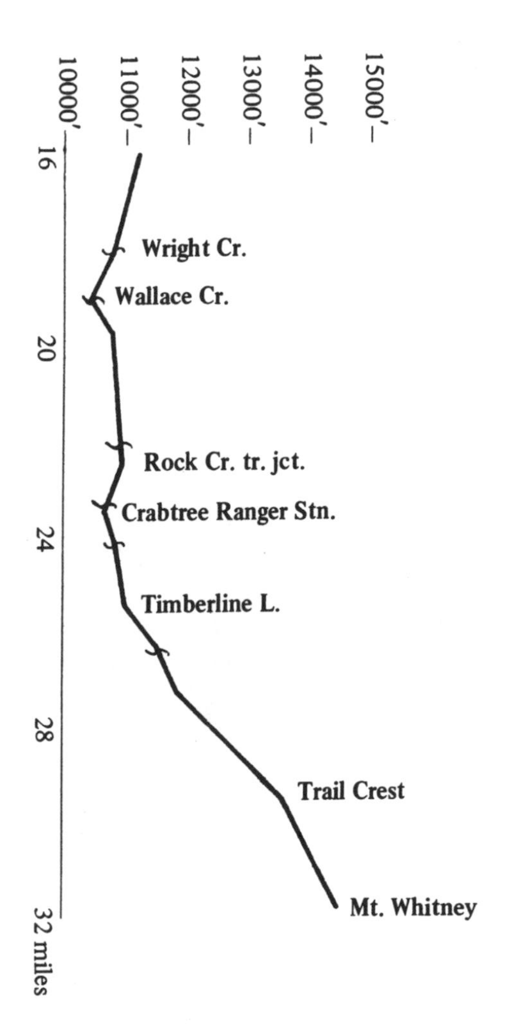
15000′
14000′
13000′
12000′
11000′
10000′
16
20
24
28
32 miles
Wright Cr.
Wallace Cr.
Rock Cr. tr. jct.
Crabtree Ranger Stn.
Timberline L.
Trail Crest
Mt. Whitney

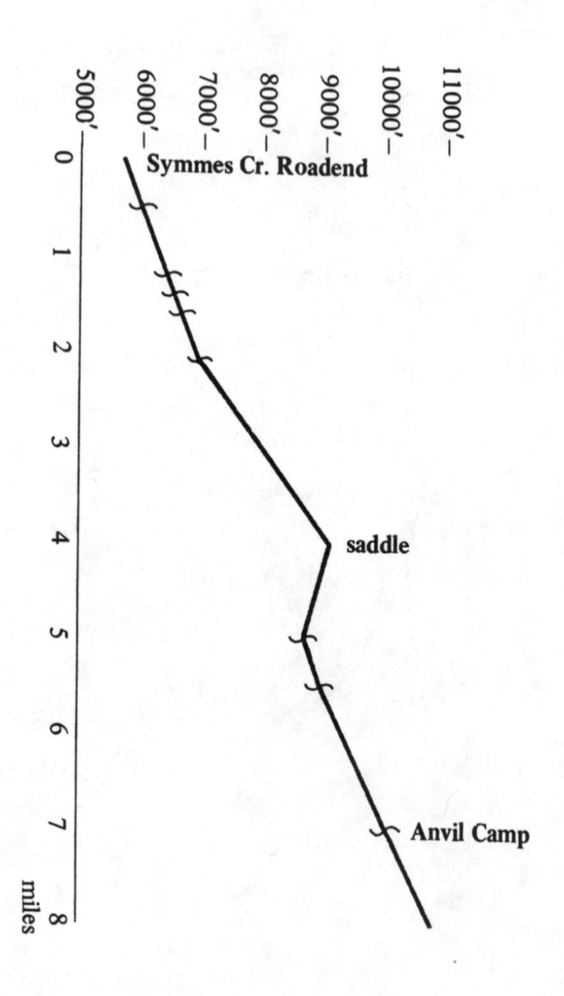
11000'
10000'
9000'
8000'
7000'
6000'
5000'
Symmes Cr. Roadend
saddle
Anvil Camp
0
1
2
3
4
5
6
7
8
miles

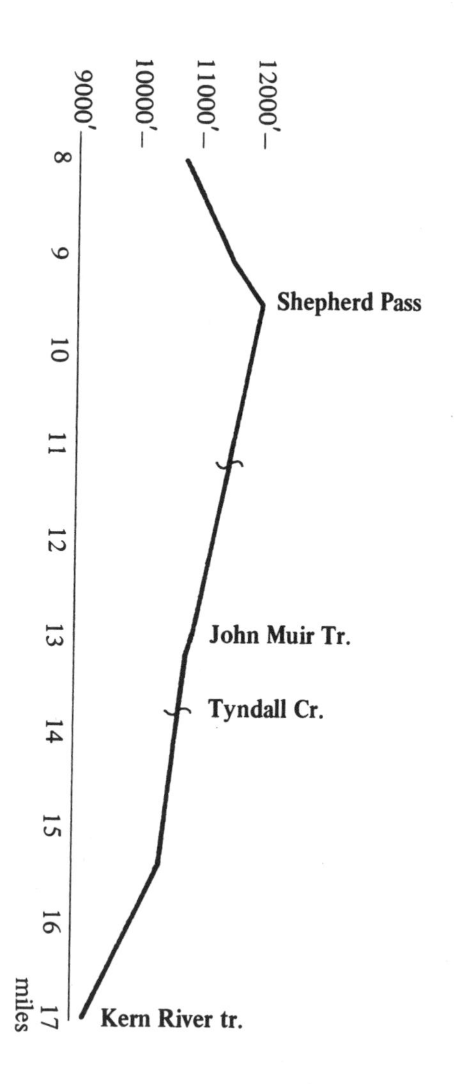
12000'
11000'
10000'
9000'
8
9
10
11
12
13
14
15
16
17
miles
Shepherd Pass
John Muir Tr.
Tyndall Cr.
Kern River tr.
Trail #2

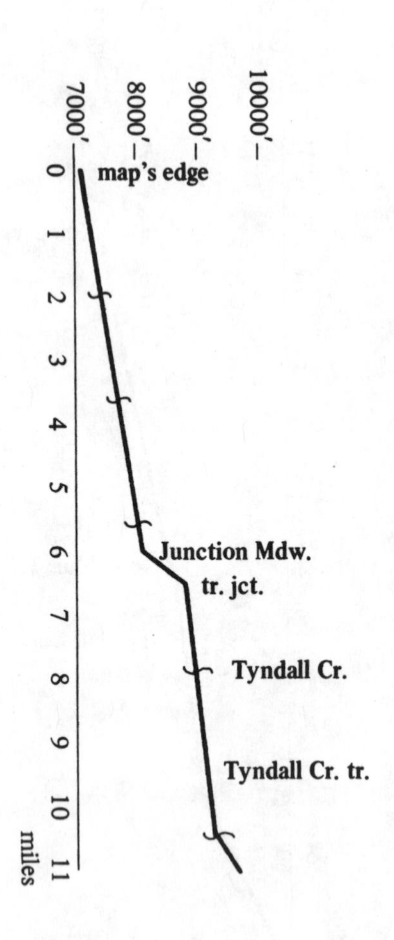
10000'
9000'
8000'
7000'
map's edge
Junction Mdw.
tr. jct.
Tyndall Cr.
Tyndall Cr. tr.
0
1
2
3
4
5
6
7
8
9
10
11
miles

Trail #3

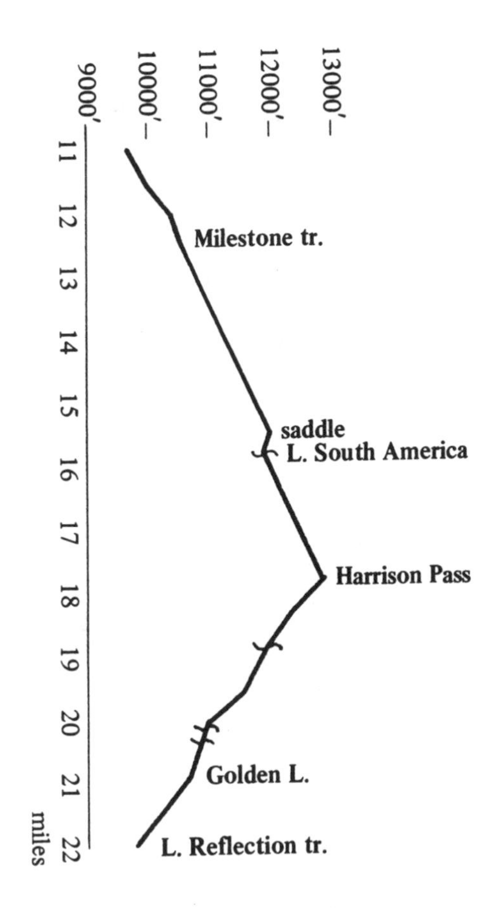
13000′
12000′
11000′
10000′
9000′
11
12
13
14
15
16
17
18
19
20
21
22
miles
Milestone tr.
saddle
L. South America
Harrison Pass
Golden L.
L. Reflection tr.

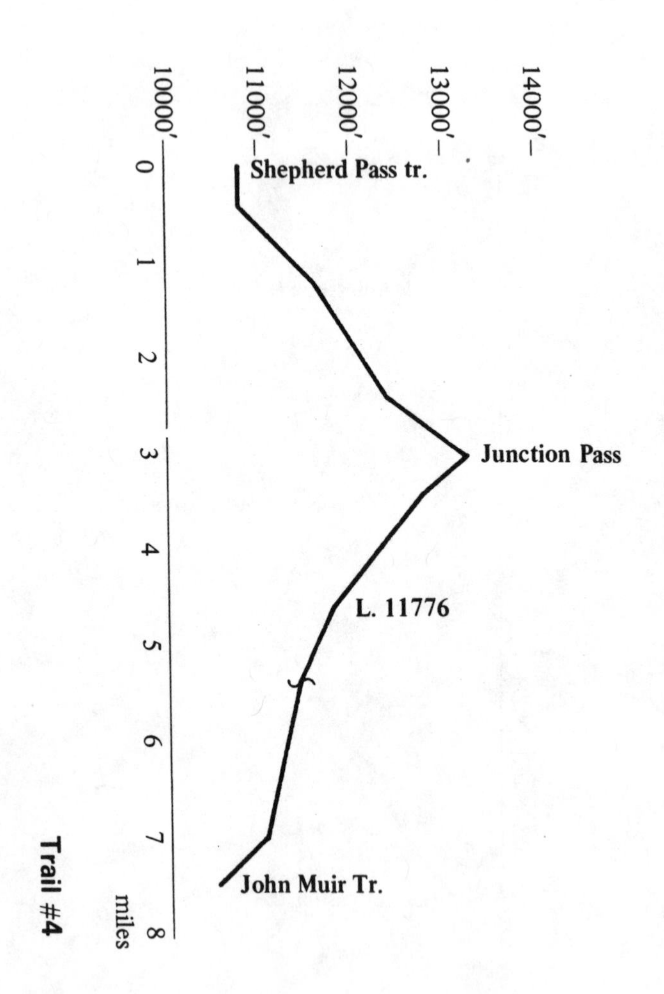
14000'
13000'
12000'
11000'
10000'
Shepherd Pass tr.
Junction Pass
L. 11776
John Muir Tr.
0
1
2
3
4
5
6
7
8
miles
Trail #4

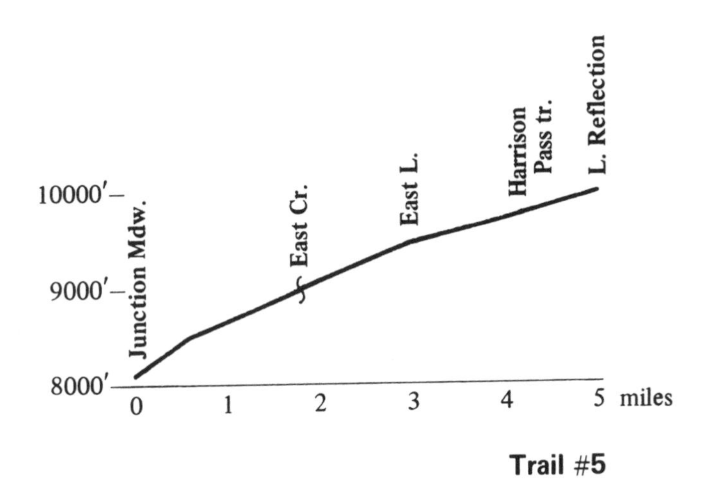

Trail #5

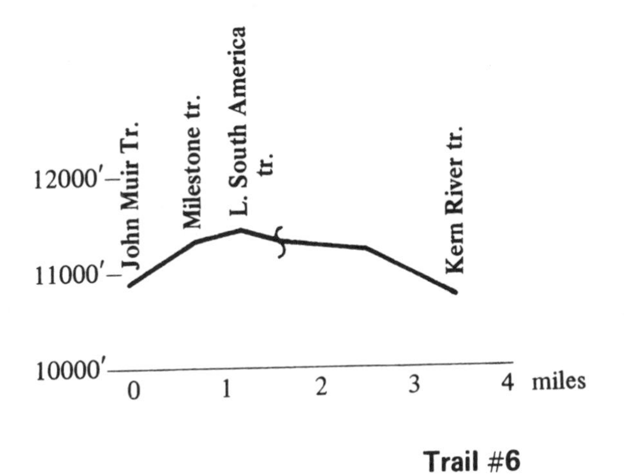

Trail #6

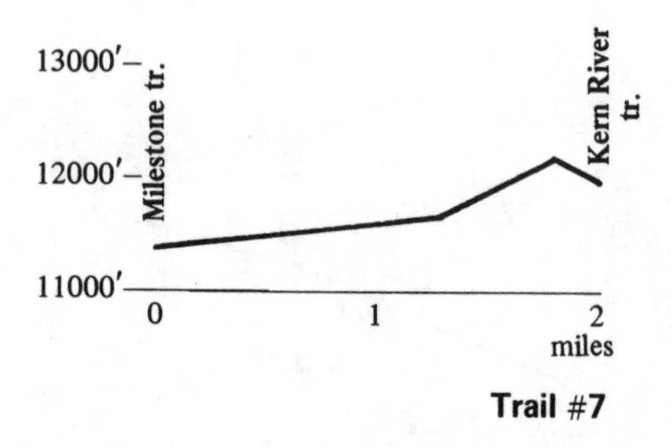

Trail #7

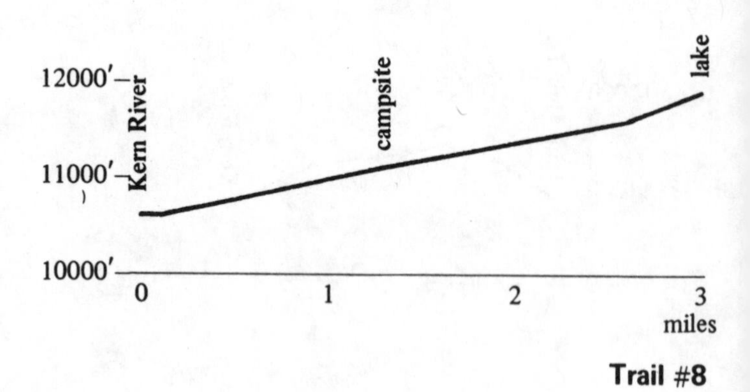

Trail #8

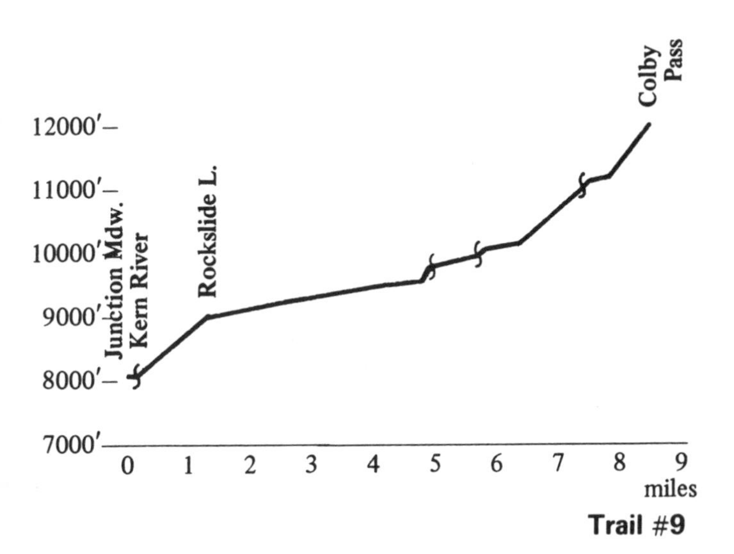
12000′
11000′
10000′
9000′
8000′
7000′
Junction Mdw.
Kern River
Rockslide L.
Colby Pass
0
1
2
3
4
5
6
7
8
9
miles
Trail #9

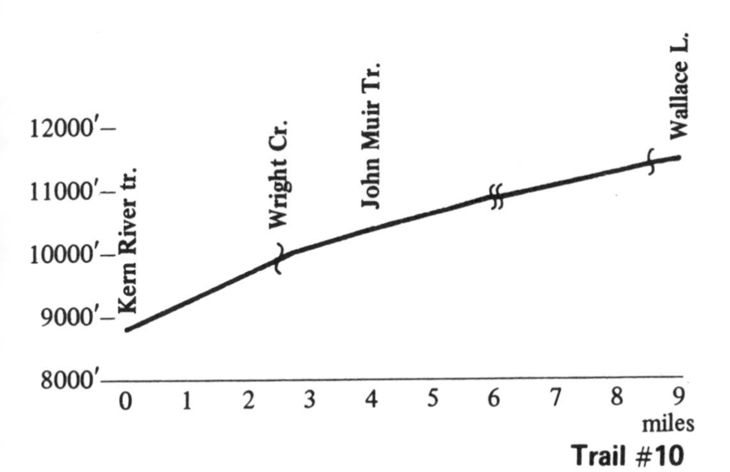
12000′
11000′
10000′
9000′
8000′
Kern River tr.
Wright Cr.
John Muir Tr.
Wallace L.
0
1
2
3
4
5
6
7
8
9
miles
Trail #10

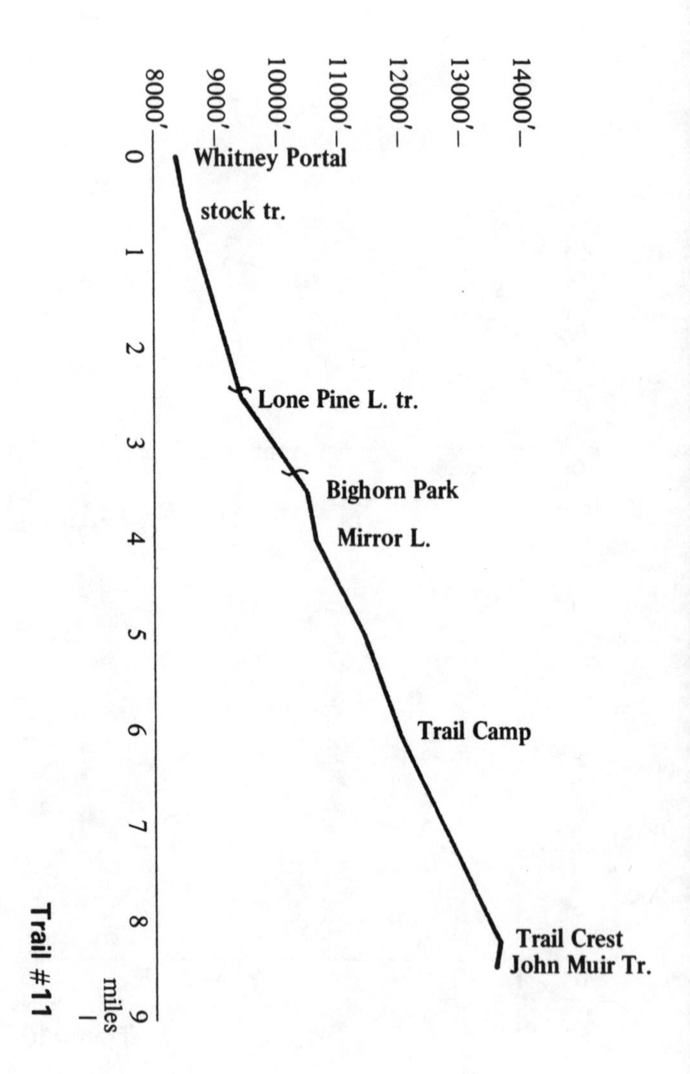
14000′
13000′
12000′
11000′
10000′
9000′
8000′
Whitney Portal
stock tr.
Lone Pine L. tr.
Bighorn Park
Mirror L.
Trail Camp
Trail Crest
John Muir Tr.
0
1
2
3
4
5
6
7
8
9
miles
Trail #11

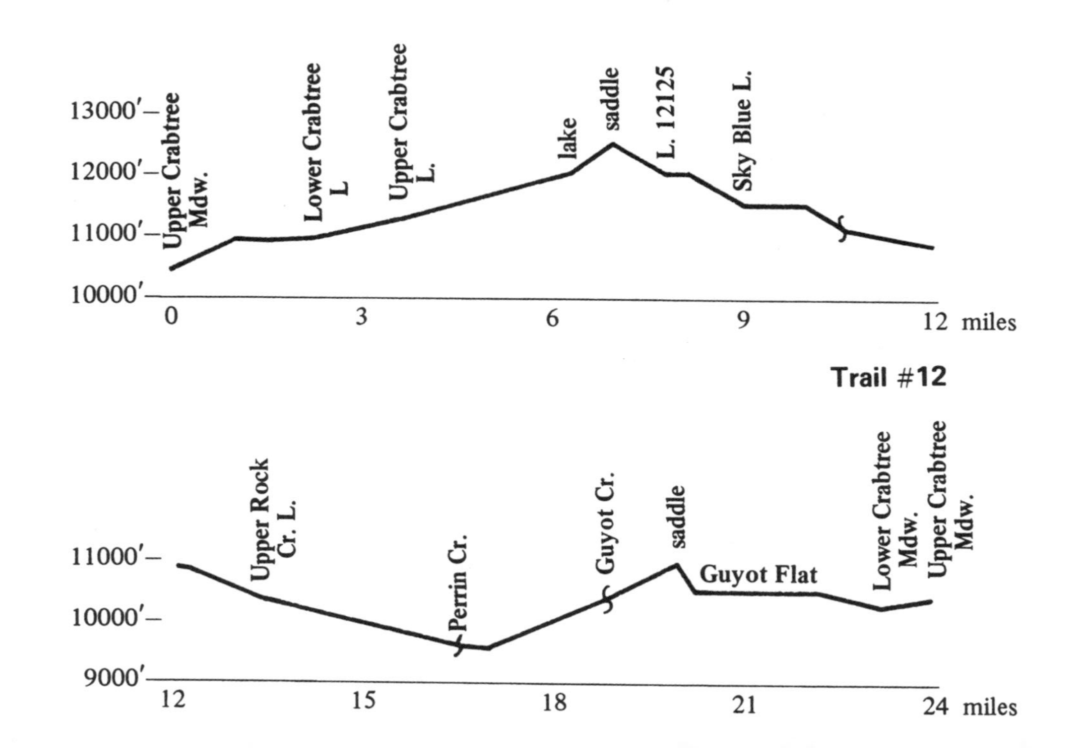
13000'
12000'
11000'
10000'
Upper Crabtree Mdw.
Lower Crabtree L
Upper Crabtree L.
lake
saddle
L. 12125
Sky Blue L.
0
3
6
9
12 miles
Trail #12
11000'
10000'
9000'
Upper Rock Cr. L.
Perrin Cr.
Guyot Cr.
saddle
Guyot Flat
Lower Crabtree Mdw.
Upper Crabtree Mdw.
12
15
18
21
24 miles

Index

Page numbers in italic type indicate photographs.